Experiencing
Poetry

**GLOBE BOOK
COMPANY**

Englewood Cliffs, New Jersey

Eileen Thompson, author and editor of language arts materials, has been involved in educational publishing for 13 years and has edited several anthologies for junior high and high school students. She began her career as a teacher and over the years has taught students from nursery school age to adults. Her abiding interest is poetry, and she is especially concerned with making poetry accessible to teenagers.

Cover Design: Berg Design

Text Design and Production: PC&F, Inc.

Photos: vi-1, Charles Harbutt/Archive; 7, Jeanne White/National Audubon Society; 10, Ira Berger/Woodfin Camp; 17, Arthur Tress/Photo Researchers; 20–21, Jean Pigozzi/Archive; 29, Michael O'Brien/Archive; 32, Tina Paul/Archive; 39, Rebecca Chao/Archive; 40–41, Cecile Brunswick/Peter Arnold; 48, Phyliss Greenberg/Photo Researchers; 57, Joern Gerdts/Photo Researchers; 63, Charles Harbutt/Archive; 66–67, Sylvia Plachy/Archive; 71, Fred Lombardi/Photo Researchers; 79, Sylvia Plachy/Archive; 85, C. G. Maxwell/Photo Researchers; 92–93, Charles Harbutt/Archive; 98, Charles Harbutt/Archive; 102, Alice Kandell/Photo Researchers; 106, Howard J. Lee/Photo Researchers; 110–11, Jill Freedman/Archive; 116, Horst Schafer/Peter Arnold; 120, Geoffrey Gove/Photo Researchers; 128–29, Roswell Angier/Archive; 133, Charles Harbutt/Archive; 138, Charles Harbutt/Archive; 142, J. Allan Cash/Rapho/Photo Researchers

Acknowledgments

ADDISON-WESLEY PUBLISHING COMPANY— for "I am Rose" by Gertrude Stein. Copyright © 1966, Addison-Wesley Publishing Company, Inc., Reading, Massachusetts. Reprinted by permission.

UNIVERSITY OF ARKANSAS PRESS— for "Interview" by Sara Henderson Hay. Reprinted from *Story Hour,* copyright © 1982 by Sara Henderson Hay.— for "Juvenile Court" by Sara Henderson. Reprinted from *Story Hour* copyright © 1982 by Sara Henderson Hay.

ATHENEUM PUBLISHERS— for "Zebra" by Judith Thurman from *Flashlight and Other Poems* by Judith Thurman. Copyright © 1976 by Judith Thurman.— for "The Island of Yorrick" by N.M. Bodecker from *Let's Marry Said the Cherry and Other Nonsense Poems.* Copyright © 1974 by N.M. Bodecker.— for "Separation" by W.S. Merwin from *The Moving Target* by W.S. Merwin. Copyright © 1960, 1962, 1963 by W.S. Merwin.— for "Something Is There" by Lilian Moore from *See My Lovely Poison Ivy* by

Lilian Moore. Copyright © 1972, 1975 by Lilian Moore.— for "Night-Piece" by Raymond R. Patterson from "Why Am I Grown So Cold?, edited by Myra Cohn Livingston. Reprinted by permission of the author and the publisher.— for "Since Hanna Moved Away" by Judith Viorst. From *If I Were In Charge of the World and Other Worries* by Judith Viorst. Copyright © 1981 by Judith Viorst.— for "Concrete Mixers" by Patricia Hubbell from *8 A.M. Shadows* by Patricia Hubbell. Copyright © 1965 by Patricia Hubbell. All selections reprinted by permission of Atheneum Publishers.

GEORGE BRAZILLER, INC.— for "Fork" by Charles Simic from *Dismantling The Silence,* © 1974.— for "Watermelons" by Charles Simic, from *Return To A Place Lit By A Glass of Milk,* © 1973.— for "Fear" by Charles Simic, from *Dismantling the Silence* by Charles Simic. Copyright © 1971 by Charles Simic. All selections reprinted by permission of George Braziller, New York.

Additional acknowledgments appear on page 149.

ISBN: 0-87065-224-9

Printed in the United States of America 9 8 7 6 5 4 3

CONTENTS

Ways of Seeing

Mirrorment, *A. R. Ammons*   2
Reflection, *Lew Sarett*   2
Zebra, *Judith Thurman*   3
Pigeons, *Lilian Moore*   4
The Sloth, *Theodore Roethke*   5
Giraffe's Laughs Last, *X. J. Kennedy*   6
My Donkey, *Ted Hughes*   8
Watermelons, *Charles Simic*   10
Fable, *Ralph Waldo Emerson*   11
Parking Lot Full, *Eve Merriam*   12
About an Excavation, *Charles Reznikoff*   12
The Closet Zoo, *Ted Kooser*   13
Fork, *Charles Simic*   14
Steam Shovel, *Charles Malam*   14
Concrete Mixers, *Patricia Hubbell*   15
Next! *Ogden Nash*   16
Cardinal Ideograms, *May Swenson*   18

Facing Yourself

Tiggady Rue, *David McCord*   22
I Am Cherry Alive, *Delmore Schwartz*   23
Everybody Says, *Dorothy Aldis*   25
Surprise, *Beverly McLoughland*   25
Me, *Walter de la Mare*   26
who are you, little i, *e.e. cummings*   26
Because, *Nikki Giovanni*   27
Mirror, *Guillaume Apollinaire*   28
Keeping Track, *Denise Levertov*   28

The Meeting, *Gerald Costanzo*   **30**
Autobiographia Literaria, *Frank O'Hara*   **31**
Miriam, *Howard Moss*   **32**
The Young Ones, Flip Side, *James A. Emanuel*   **33**
The Delight Song of Tsoai-Talee,
    N. Scott Momaday   **34**
Africa, *Lucille Clifton*   **36**
Who Can Be Born Black, *Mari Evans*   **36**
How a Girl Got Her Chinese Name, *Nellie Wong*   **38**

Reaching Out

Oath of Friendship, *Anonymous*   **42**
Sing a Song of People, *Lois Lenski*   **43**
The Hero, *Robert Graves*   **45**
Together, *Paul Engle*   **46**
Valentine, *Donald Hall*   **46**
My Valentine, *Robert Louis Stevenson*   **47**
Sunday, *James Schuyler*   **48**
A Birthday, *Christina Rossetti*   **48**
The Invention of the Telephone, *Peter Klappert*   **50**
If You Have Had Your Midnights, *Mari Evans*   **51**
love is more thicker than forget, *e.e. cummings*   **52**
After the Rain, *Paul B. Janeczko*   **53**
When You Laugh, *Ingrid Jonker*   **53**
Jenny Kiss'd Me, *Leigh Hunt*   **54**
Senses of Insecurity, *Maya Angelou*   **55**
Pocket Poem, *Ted Kooser*   **56**
On Being Introduced to You, *Eve Merriam*   **58**
First Lesson, *Philip Booth*   **59**
Little Elegy for a child who skipped rope,
    X. J. Kennedy   **60**
Legacies, *Nikki Giovanni*   **61**
The Harp, *Bruce Weigl*   **62**
Herbs in the Attic, *Marilyn Waniek*   **64**

Sudden Surprises

Fancy Dive, *Shel Silverstein*   **68**
Blue Alert, *Eve Merriam*   **69**
Waking from a Nap on the Beach, *May Swenson*   **70**
The First Salad of March, *Marge Piercy*   **72**
Strawberries, *Judith Hemschemeyer*   **74**
The Bagel, *David Ignatow*   **76**
Lord Cray, *Edward Gorey*   **77**
Flight of the Roller-Coaster, *Raymond Souster*   **78**
Little Red Riding Hood and the Wolf, *Roald Dahl*   **80**
Reflections Dental, *Phyllis McGinley*   **82**
Simultaneously, *David Ignatow*   **83**
April 5, 1974, *Richard Wilbur*   **84**
Mushrooms, *Sylvia Plath*   **86**
Mushrooms, *Mary Oliver*   **88**
Geometry, *Rita Dove*   **90**
Books Fall Open, *David McCord*   **91**

Saying Good-bye

Housecleaning, *Nikki Giovanni*   **94**
Since Hanna Moved Away, *Judith Viorst*   **95**
Separation, *W. S. Merwin*   **96**
Separation, *P. Wolny*   **96**
Poem, *Langston Hughes*   **97**
The Opposite of Two, *Richard Wilbur*   **97**
The Departure, *Frank Steele*   **98**
Goodbye, *Sherod Santos*   **99**
So, We'll Go No More A-Roving, *Lord Byron*   **100**
Music, When Soft Voices Die,
   Percy Bysshe Shelley   **101**
Miss Blues'es Child, *Langston Hughes*   **102**
No Labor-Savings Machine, *Walt Whitman*   **103**
For Laurie, *May Sarton*   **104**
Acquainted with the Night, *Robert Frost*   **105**

Something Told the Wild Geese, *Rachel Field*   **106**
Wild Goose, *Curtis Heath*   **107**
Little Things, *James Stephens*   **108**
Splinter, *Carl Sandburg*   **108**
One Day in August, *William Stafford*   **109**

Green Places and Other Delights

from Auguries of Innocence, *William Blake*   **112**
Walking in the Rain, *Dan Saxon*   **113**
Daybreak in Alabama, *Langston Hughes*   **114**
March, *Elizabeth Coatsworth*   **115**
Beyond Winter, *Ralph Waldo Emerson*   **115**
Pippa's Passing, *Robert Browning*   **116**
I Think, *James Schuyler*   **117**
Knoxville, Tennessee, *Nikki Giovanni*   **118**
Road, *W. S. Merwin*   **119**
Sound of Rapids of Laramie River in Late August,
   W. S. Merwin   **119**
Dust of Snow, *Robert Frost*   **120**
A Green Place, *William Jay Smith*   **121**
A Blessing, *James Wright*   **122**
The Peace of Wild Things, *Wendell Berry*   **123**
The Waking, *Theodore Roethke*   **124**
Fog, *Carl Sandburg*   **125**
Fog, *William Jay Smith*   **125**
The quiet fog, *Marge Piercy*   **126**
The City, *David Ignatow*   **127**
City, *Langston Hughes*   **127**

That Enchanted Kingdom

Otherwise, *Aileen Fisher*   **130**
Witchcraft was hung, in History,
   Emily Dickinson   **130**
The White Horse, *D. H. Lawrence*   **131**

from Kubla Khan, *Samuel Taylor Coleridge*   **132**
Sleeping Beauty, *Walter de la Mare*   **133**
La Belle Dame sans Merci, *John Keats*   **134**
Independent Testimony, *Charles Simic*   **136**
Interview, *Sara Henderson Hay*   **137**
Haiku, *Issa and Joso*   **138**
Long Distance, *William Stafford*   **139**
The Secret, *James Stephens*   **140**
Southern Mansion, *Arna Bontemps*   **141**
The Island of Yorrick, *N. M. Bodecker*   **142**
All Hallows, *Louise Glück*   **143**
Night-Piece, *Raymond R. Patterson*   **144**
from The Raven, *Edgar Allan Poe*   **145**
Poem, *Southwest Tribes*   **145**
Something Is There, *Lilian Moore*   **146**
Fear, *Charles Simic*   **146**
Moon Tiger, *Denise Levertov*   **147**
Where the Sidewalk Ends, *Shel Silverstein*   **148**

A fool sees not the same tree as a wise man sees.

William Blake

Ways of Seeing

How is a reflection different from the original?

Mirrorment _____

A. R. Ammons

Birds are flowers flying
and flowers perched birds.

Reflection _____

Lew Sarett

Beauty is a lily,
Sparkling and cool,
It's a bowl of dewy petals
Stemming in a pool.

Meditate on beauty,
Hold it, and look!—
Beauty shall be doubled,—
A lily in a brook.

Zebra

Judith Thurman

white sun
black
fire escape,

morning
grazing like a zebra
outside my window.

RESPONDING

1. In the first poem, the poet sees the similarity between birds and flowers. (a) When you look closely at birds, in what way do they resemble flowers? (b) When you look closely at flowers, in what way do they resemble birds?

2. In the second poem, the poet looks at a lily and sees beauty. Why will beauty be doubled if the lily is in a brook?

3. In the third poem, what remarkable sight does the poet see when she looks at the sun shining through the fire escape?

WRITING

A reflection is very like the original, but also very different. For example, when you see it in a mirror, the letter *b* looks like the letter *d* and a clock seems to run backward. Select a familiar object. Hold it up to a mirror. Think about it. Then write a two-line poem describing what you see.

How are pigeons like city folk?

Pigeons

Lilian Moore

Pigeons are city folk
content
to live with concrete
and cement.

They seldom
spy
the sky.

A pigeon never sings
of dell

and flowering hedge,
but busily commutes
from sidewalk
to his ledge.

Oh pigeon, what a waste of
wings!

RESPONDING

1. The poet compares pigeons to city folk. In what way are people living in the city like pigeons?

2. In what way are pigeons not like other birds?

3. After considering pigeons, the poet forms an opinion about them. She writes, "Oh pigeon, what a waste of wings!" (a) What does she mean by this statement? (b) In what way does this verdict apply to city folk as well?

WRITING

Usually we think of the city in terms of buildings, not of animals. However, many animals do live there. Brainstorm to develop a list of city creatures. Then select one as your topic. Finally, write a short poem expressing your opinion of this creature.

How would the world look from upside down?

The Sloth _____

Theodore Roethke

In moving-slow he has no Peer.
You ask him something in his ear;
He thinks about it for a Year;

And, then, before he says a Word
There, upside down (unlike a Bird)
He will assume that you have Heard—

A most Ex-as-per-at-ing Lug.
But should you call his manner Smug,
He'll sigh and give his Branch a Hug.

Then off again to Sleep he goes,
Still swaying gently by his Toes,
And you just *know* he knows he knows.

RESPONDING

What impression do you form of the sloth from reading this poem?

WRITING

Roethke wrote his poem in three-line *stanzas,* or groups of lines. In each stanza, the words at the end of lines rhyme. For example, in the first stanza, *Peer, ear,* and *Year* all rhyme.

Brainstorm to develop a list of unusual animals. Select one. Decide what impression you want to create. Using three-line stanzas in which the words at the end of lines rhyme, write a poem describing this creature's behavior.

What does the giraffe see when it looks at you?

Giraffe's Laughs Last_____

X.J. Kennedy

When spied on in a zoo, Giraffe
　Neglects his treeleaf diet
To take a look at you and laugh—
　Your short neck! What a riot!

If he should grin from ear to ear
　And you've not yet departed,
In several weeks you'll get to hear
　The throaty laugh you started.

RESPONDING

1. When we look at the giraffe, we see its long neck as odd, or unusual. According to this poem, how does the giraffe view our short necks?

2. Why does it take several weeks to hear the giraffe's laugh?

WRITING

This poem is written in two stanzas. Study the rhyme scheme in each stanza. Then write a paragraph analyzing this scheme.

Do some creatures put a smile on your face?

My Donkey ──────────────

Ted Hughes

Is an ancient color. He's the color
Of a prehistoric desert
Where great prehistoric suns have sunk and burned out
To a bluish powder.

He stood there through it all, head hanging.

He's the color
Of a hearth full of ashes, next morning,
Tinged with rusty pink.

Or the color of a cast-iron donkey, roasted in a bonfire,
And still standing there after it, cooling,
Pale with ashes and oxides.

He's been through a lot.
But here he is in the nettles, under the chestnut leaves,
With his surprising legs—
Such useful ready legs, so light and active—

And neat round hooves, for putting down just anywhere,
Ready to start out again this minute scrambling all over
   Tibet!

And his quite small body, tough and tight and useful,
Like traveller's luggage,
A thing specially made for hard use, with no trimmings,
Nearly ugly. Made to outlast its owner.

His face is what I like.
And his head, much too big for his body—a toy head,
A great, rabbit-eared, pantomime head—
And his friendly rabbit face,

His big, friendly, humorous eyes, which can turn wicked,
Long and devilish, when he lays his ears back.

But mostly he's comical—and that's what I like.
I like the joke he seems
Always just about to tell me. And the laugh,

The rusty pump-house engine that cranks up laughter
From some long-ago, far-off, laughterless desert—

The dry, hideous guffaw
That makes his great teeth nearly fall out.

RESPONDING

1. The poet creates an impression of the donkey as a survivor. What words indicate that the donkey has been around for a good long time?

2. Obviously, the poet admires the donkey, but the donkey's appearance also arouses another feeling in him. (a) What is this feeling? (b) What details does the poet use to make you feel this way about the donkey, too?

WRITING

Some animals just make us feel good. For example, for some people nothing is so pleasant as a cat sitting in their lap. Is there an animal that puts a smile on your face even after a difficult day? (It might even be a stuffed animal from childhood or an animated creature on television.) Use this animal as your topic. Then write a poem describing the special way in which you see this creature.

What do you see when you look at a row of watermelons?

Watermelons

Charles Simic

Green Buddhas
On the fruit stand.
We eat the smile
And spit out the teeth.

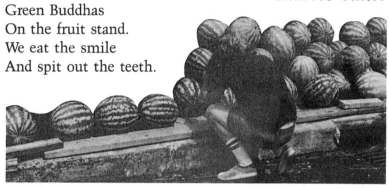

RESPONDING

1. Statues of the Buddha, the Indian philosopher and sage, usually portray a big, round fellow sitting with legs crossed, serenely considering the universe. How are watermelons like statues of the Buddha?

2. (a) The poet says we "eat the smile." What are we really eating? (b) He says we "spit out the teeth." What are we really spitting out?

WRITING

The poet uses a *metaphor*—a comparison between two basically unlike things—to create a vivid picture of watermelons. Choose a common, everyday object such as a scouring pad or a tea kettle or a television set. Look at it carefully. What comparisons spring to mind? Then, using a metaphor to describe it, write a four-line poem.

Is anything really insignificant?

Fable

Ralph Waldo Emerson

The mountain and the squirrel
Had a quarrel;
And the former called the latter "Little Prig."
Bun replied,
"You are doubtless very big;
But all sorts of things and weather
Must be taken in together
To make up a year
And a sphere."

RESPONDING

1. Who are the speakers in this poem?

2. A *fable* usually teaches a lesson for living. What lesson does this poem teach?

WRITING

Sometimes we look at very large things and, because of their size, see them as more important than smaller things. However, looks can be deceiving. For example, the microscopic bacteria can fell the mightiest king.

   Brainstorm to form a list of tiny creatures or objects that are really quite important or powerful. Choose one as your topic. Then write a short poem in the form of a fable explaining the might of this creature or object.

What do you see when you look at city sites?

Parking Lot Full _____

Eve Merriam

a much of motors
an over of drives
a choke of carburetors
a flood of engines

a plethora of wheels
a googol of gas tanks
a total of exhausts

About an Excavation _____

Charles Reznikoff

About an excavation
a flock of bright red lanterns
has settled.

RESPONDING

1. *Diction* refers to word choice. In the first poem, the
   poet chooses words carefully to create a vivid
   impression of a full parking lot. Which words create
   the effect of a superabundance of everything?

2. In the second poem, the poet finds beauty in everyday
   things. (a) To what does he compare the red lanterns?
   (b) How are these two items alike?

WRITING

In writing "Parking Lot Full," Eve Merriam had each line
follow this scheme: a _____ of _____ .
Following this pattern, write a poem creating a particular
impression of an ordinary city sight.

What do you see when you open the door to your closet?

The Closet Zoo

Ted Kooser

In the closet zoo, umbrella bats
hang upside-down to dry their wings,
and the Samsonite rhinoceros
watches the hatbird snatching straw
from the easy-going broom-giraffe.
And high above, in the hanger-vines,
where the clothespin parrots perch to talk,
the wool gorillas swing away
past necktie snakes and muffler sloths;
they make the sportcoat gibbons hoot
with wonder in the closet zoo.

RESPONDING

1. The poet compares his closet with a zoo. (a) In what way are umbrellas like bats? (b) In what way is a Samsonite suitcase like a rhinoceros?

2. (a) What object in his closet does he call a hatbird? (b) How is a broom like a giraffe?

3. An *extended metaphor* is one that is carried through the entire poem. Do you think the poet's comparing the closet to the zoo is effective? Why or why not?

WRITING

Open the door to your closet. Look at it carefully. What do you see? Using an extended metaphor, write a poem describing your closet.

When you look at a common, everyday object out of the corner of your eye, does it seem to come alive?

Fork

Charles Simic

This strange thing must have crept
Right out of hell.
It resembles a bird's foot
Worn around the cannibal's neck.

As you hold it in your hand,
As you stab with it into a piece of meat,
It is possible to imagine the rest of the bird:
Its head which like your fist
Is large, bald, beakless and blind.

Steam Shovel

Charles Malam

The dinosaurs are not all dead.
I saw one raise its iron head
To watch me walking down the road
Beyond our house today.
Its jaws were dripping with a load
Of earth and grass that it had cropped.
It must have heard me where I stopped,
Snorted white steam my way,
And stretched its long neck out to see,
And chewed, and grinned quite amiably.

Concrete Mixers

Patricia Hubbell

The drivers are washing the concrete mixers;
Like elephant tenders they hose them down.
Tough gray-skinned monsters standing ponderous,
Elephant-bellied and elephant-nosed,
Standing in muck up to their wheel-caps,
Like rows of elephants, tail to trunk.
Their drivers perch on their backs like mahouts,
Sending the sprays of water up.
They rid the trunk-like trough of concrete,
Direct the spray to the bulging sides,
Turn and start the monsters moving.
                    Concrete mixers
                    Move like elephants
                    Bellow like elephants
                    Spray like elephants,
        Concrete mixers are urban elephants.
        Their trunks are raising a city.

RESPONDING

1. In the first poem, the poet sees a fork as a devilish object. In what way is it like some fearsome bird?

2. In the second poem, to what does the poet compare the steam shovel?

3. A *simile* compares basically unlike things by using the word *like* or *as*. In the third poem, to what does the poet compare the concrete mixers?

WRITING

Think about the machines you use every day. Select one. Using similes, write a poem describing it.

What would happen if the fossils in a natural history museum came alive?

Next! _____

Ogden Nash

I thought that I would like to see
The early world that used to be,
That mastodonic mausoleum,
The Natural History Museum.
At midnight in the vasty hall
The fossils gathered for a ball.
High above notices and bulletins
Loomed up the Mesozoic skeletons.
Aroused by who knows what elixirs,
They ground along like concrete mixers.

They bowed and scraped in reptile pleasure,
And then began to tread the measure.
There were no drums or saxophones,
But just the clatter of their bones,
A rolling, rattling carefree circus
Of mammoth polkas and mazurkas.
Pterodactyls and brontosauruses
Sang ghostly prehistoric choruses.
Amid the megalosauric wassail
I caught the eye of one small fossil.
Cheer up, old man, he said, and winked—
It's kind of fun to be extinct.

RESPONDING

1. In this delightful poem, the poet sees the fossils in the Natural History Museum coming to life at night. (a) What do they do once they are animated? (b) What do they use for music?

2. What *mood*, or feeling, does this poem create?

WRITING

Part of the fun of reading this poem is trying not to trip over the words. Notice all the words that are a delight to say: for example, *mastodonic mausoleum, Mesozoic skeletons, mammoth polkas and mazurkas,* and *megalosauric wassail.*

Imagine what would happen if an art museum were to come alive. Write a poem describing the scene. Try to include in your poem words that are fun to say. For example, you might describe a woman as dancing in her *Rubenesque rotundity.*

17

What do you see when you look at numerals?

Cardinal Ideograms _____

May Swenson

0   A mouth. Can blow or breathe,
    be funnel, or Hello.

1   A grass blade or a cut.

2   A question seated. And a proud
    bird's neck.

3   Shallow mitten for two-fingered hand.

4   Three-cornered hut
    on one stilt. Sometimes built
    so the roof gapes.

5   A policeman. Polite.
    Wearing visored cap.

6   O unrolling,
    tape of ambiguous length
    on which is written the mystery
    of everything curly.

7   A step,
    detached from its stair.

8   The universe in diagram:
    A cosmic hourglass.
    (Note enigmatic shape,
    absence of any valve of origin,
    how end overlaps beginning.)
    Unknotted like a shoelace
    and whipped back and forth,
    can serve as a model of time.

Lorgnette for the right eye.
9   In England or if you are Alice
the stem is on the left.

A grass blade or a cut
10 companioned by a mouth.
Open? Open. Shut? Shut.

RESPONDING

May Swenson looked at the cardinal numerals and saw pictures, or ideograms. Which image did you find most effective? Why?

WRITING

Look at the first five letters of the alphabet. Following the pattern of "Cardinal Ideograms", describe each of these letters.

Not in the clamor of the crowded street.
Not in the shouts and plaudits of the throng,
But in ourselves, are triumphs and defeat.

Henry Wadsworth Longfellow

Facing
Yourself

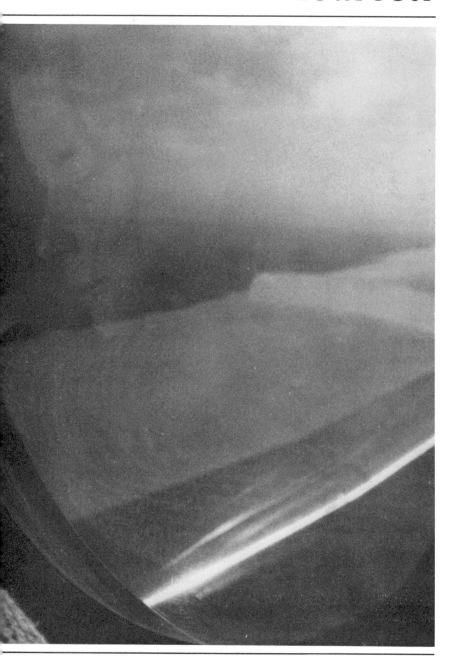

How would you feel if someone could see into your heart?

Tiggady Rue

David McCord

Curious, curious Tiggady Rue
Looks and looks in the heart of you;
She finds you good,
She finds you bad,
Generous, mean,
Grumpy, glad—
Tiggady Rue.

Curious, curious Tiggady Rue
Tells your thoughts and tells you *you;*
Elephant thoughts,
And spry and lean,
And thoughts made like a jumping bean,
Or wedgy ones
Slid in between—
She knows them, too,
If she looks at you,
Tiggady Rue.

Curious, curious Tiggady Rue
Knows your thoughts and you and you.
When dusk is down
On field and town,
Beware!
Take care!
If she looks at you—
Tiggady Rue.

I Am Cherry Alive

Delmore Schwartz

"I am cherry alive," the little girl sang,
"Each morning I am something new:
I am apple, I am plum, I am just as excited
As the boys who made the Hallowe'en bang:
I am tree, I am cat, I am blossom too:
When I like, if I like, I can be someone new,
Someone very old, a witch in a zoo:
I can be someone else whenever I think who,
And I want to be everything sometimes too:
And the peach has a pit and I know that too,
And I put it in along with everything
To make the grown-ups laugh whenever I sing:
And I sing: *It is true; It is untrue;*
I know, I know, the true is untrue,
The peach has a pit,
The pit has a peach:
And both may be wrong
When I sing my song,
But I don't tell the grown-ups: because it is sad,
And I want them to laugh just like I do
Because they grew up
And forgot what they knew
And they are sure
I will forget it some day too.
They are wrong. They are wrong.

When I sang my song, I knew, I knew!
I am red, I am gold,
I am green, I am blue,
I will always be me,
I will always be new!"

RESPONDING

1. In the first poem, what is Tiggady Rue's special power?

2. Which words tell you that Tiggady Rue sees that you have thoughts and dreams of many different types?

3. This poem ends on a cautionary note. Why does the poet tell you to beware?

4. The *speaker* in "I Am Cherry Alive" is a young girl. What does her imagination allow her to do that adults cannot do?

5. The girl says, "And the peach has a pit and I know that too." What does this line mean?

6. (a) According to the girl, what did the grown-ups forget? (b) What will she never forget?

WRITING

Are you someone filled with contradictions? Are you someone with a sure and steady path ahead of you? Are you brave and strong? Are you meek and timid? Are you all these things? Write a song of yourself, telling who you are.

Is there a hidden you that no one knows?

Everybody Says

Dorothy Aldis

Everybody says
I look just like my mother.
Everybody says
I'm the image of Aunt Bee.

Everybody says
My nose is like my father's,
But *I* want to look like *me*.

Surprise

Beverly McLoughland

The biggest
Surprise
On the library shelf
Is when you suddenly
Find yourself

Inside a book—
(The *hidden* you)
You wonder how
The author knew.

RESPONDING

1. In the first poem, people compare the child to other members of her family. Who does the child want to be like?
2. The second poem claims that a big surprise awaits you. (a) Where can you find this surprise? (b) What is it?

WRITING

Starting with the first line, every other line in Aldis's poem consists of the words "Everybody says." However, the last line breaks this pattern. Think about the meaning of the last line. Then write a paragraph explaining what reason the poet might have had for breaking the pattern.

How does life go on after the cycle of seasons is completed?

Me
Walter de la Mare

As long as I live
I shall always be
My Self—and no other,
Just me.

Like a tree—
Willow, elder,
Aspen, thorn,
Or cypress forlorn.

Like a flower,
For its hour—

Primrose, or pink,
Or a violet—
Sunned by the sun,
And with dewdrops wet.

Always just me.
Till the day come on
When I leave this body,
It's all then done,
And the spirit within it
Is gone.

who are you, little i
e. e. cummings

who are you, little i

(five or six years old)
peering from some high

window;at the gold

of november sunset

(and feeling:that if day
has to become night

this is a beautiful way)

26

BECAUSE

Nikki Giovanni

i wrote a poem
for you because
you are
my little boy

i wrote a poem
for you because
you are
my darling daughter

and in this poem
i sang a song
that says
as time goes on
i am you
and you are me
and that's how life
goes on

RESPONDING

1. In "Me" the speaker asserts that he will always be
   himself. (a) To what does he compare himself?
   (b) Choose three of these comparisons and tell why
   they are effective.

2. (a) To whom is the second poem addressed? In other
   words, to whom is the speaker talking? (b) What is the
   meaning of the last three lines of this poem?

3. (a) What reason does the poet give for writing
   "Because"? (b) In what way is the poet her children and
   her children her?

WRITING

These three poems share the same topic—the changing
seasons of life. First identify the *theme*, or central
meaning, of each. Then write a paragraph comparing and
contrasting the themes.

What do you see when you look in the mirror?

Mirror

Guillaume Apollinaire

```
                IN
          IONS  THIS
       FLECT        MIR
       RE           ROR
       THE            I
       LIKE  Guillaume  AM
       NOT  Apollinaire  EN
       AND          CLOSED
       GELS           A
       AN            LIVE
        GINE        AND
         MA        REAL
          I      AS
            YOU
```

Keeping Track

Denise Levertov

Between chores—
        hulling strawberries,
        answering letters—
or between poems,

returning to the mirror
to see if I'm there.

RESPONDING

1. Instead of reading from left to right, the words in the first poem read in a circle, starting with the top word. Read this poem aloud. Where does the poem end?

2. (a) In the second poem, why does the poet return to the mirror? (b) Why does she call the poem "Keeping Track"?

WRITING

Guillaume Apollinaire's poem "Mirror" is a good example of a *concrete poem*, a poem that looks like what it is about. The words form the frame of the mirror, and the poet's name takes the place of his reflection. Make a list of topics for concrete poems; for example, a mailbox, a bicycle, a tulip, a dog. Then write a short poem describing your topic. Finally, arrange the words so that they form a physical picture of your topic.

Have you ever suddenly come face-to-face with yourself?

The Meeting _____

Gerald Costanzo

Somewhere along the road
you meet up with yourself.
Recognition is immediate.
If it happens at the proper
time and place, you propose
a toast:

May you remain as my shadow
                    when I lie down.
May I live on as your ghost.

Then you pass, knowing you'll
never see yourself that way
again: the fires which burn
before you are your penance,
the ashes you leave behind are
your name.

RESPONDING

(a) Do you infer that the poet considers self-recognition,
or understanding of oneself, good or bad? (b) Which
details support your inference?

WRITING

When you *paraphrase*, you restate the meaning of a
passage in other words to clarify its meaning. Think
carefully about "The Meeting." Look especially at the last
four lines. Then paraphrase the poem's meaning.

Do you find yourself becoming more open to wonderment and joy?

Autobiographia Literaria

Frank O'Hara

When I was a child
I played by myself in a
corner of the schoolyard
all alone.

I hated dolls and I
hated games, animals were
not friendly and birds
flew away.

If anyone was looking
for me I hid behind a
tree and cried out "I am
an orphan."

And here I am, the
center of all beauty!
writing these poems!
Imagine!

RESPONDING

1. Childhood is considered a time of wonderment and joy. What details does the poet give to show that his childhood was unusual?

2. A poet is one who can appreciate the beauty and magic in life. Why is it amazing that this child grew into a poet?

3. (a) How does the poet feel about this transformation, or change? (b) Which lines support your answer?

WRITING

This poem is written in *free verse*—verse that is free of regular patterns of rhythm and rhyme. Using free verse, write a short poem about a transformation you have undergone.

Have you ever looked at yourself as though you were playing a part in a movie?

Miriam

Howard Moss

Her long legs stepped across the furniture
And into another world. There stood
A tall girl stepping over furniture
And into another world. Was she
The movie she was watching? Or was she
The girl she watched, watching the movie?
Either way it was "The Miriam Story"
Played by Miriam who was writing the story
Of Miriam playing "The Miriam Story."

The dialogue should have gone like this,
The monologue ("I mean") should have gone like this:

"If you accept me, I will turn away.
If you reject me, I will turn toward you.
I feel so much. Touch me if you can.
And, oh, if I say no, please try again."

RESPONDING

In what way does "Miriam" reveal the total self-absorption of youth?

WRITING

A *conundrum* is a problem that has no satisfactory solution. Write a paragraph explaining in what way "Miriam" is a conundrum.

Does youth sometimes hurt?

The Young Ones, Flip Side ___

James A. Emanuel

In tight pants, tight skirts,
stretched or squeezed,
youth hurts.
Crammed in, bursting out,
Flesh will sing
And hide its doubt
In nervous hips, hopping glance,
Usurping rouge,
Provoking stance.

Put off, or put on,
Youth hurts. And then
It's gone.

RESPONDING

1. According to the poem, in what way is youth like the clothing young poeple wear?

2. (a) How does youth hide this hurt? (b) What happens after youth stops hurting?

WRITING

This poem about youth is written from the perspective of someone who is an adult. Now it's your turn. Write a short poem about adults from the perspective of youth.

Are you in tune with the natural world?

The Delight Song of Tsoai-Talee

N. Scott Momaday

I am a feather in the bright sky.
I am the blue horse that runs in the plain.
I am the fish that rolls, shining, in the water.
I am the shadow that follows a child.
I am the evening light, the lustre of meadows.
I am an eagle playing with the wind.
I am a cluster of bright beads.
I am the farthest star.
I am the cold of the dawn.
I am the roaring of the rain.
I am the glitter on the crust of the snow.
I am the long track of the moon in a lake.
I am a flame of four colors.
I am a deer standing away in the dusk.
I am a field of sumac and the pomme blanche.
I am an angle of geese upon the winter sky.
I am the hunger of a young wolf.
I am the whole dream of these things.

You see, I am alive, I am alive.
I stand in good relation to the earth.
I stand in good relation to the gods.
I stand in good relation to all that is beautiful.
I stand in good relation to the daughter of Tsen-tainte.
You see, I am alive, I am alive.

RESPONDING

1. Tsoai-Talee is the tribal name of N. Scott Momaday. In his "delight song," Momaday takes great pleasure in identifying with many objects. Choose three of these objects and explain why they might fill him with joy.

2. Tsoai-Talee enjoys being alive. (a) To what does he stand in good relation? (b) Why is this important?

WRITING

Write your own "delight song." Begin each line of the poem with the words "I am."

Do you take pride in your heritage?

Africa
Lucille Clifton

home
oh
home
the soul of your
variety
all of my bones
remember

Who Can Be Born Black
Mari Evans

Who
can be born black
and not
sing
the wonder of it
the joy
the
challenge

Who
can be born
black
and not exult!

RESPONDING

1. In the first poem, the speaker considers Africa her home, although she was not born there. How does she remember Africa?

2. According to the second poem, how should people who have been born black react to their blackness?

3. (a) What wonder do you think the poet sees in being born black? (b) What joy does she see? (c) What challenge does she see?

WRITING

Think about your ancestral home, the place where your ancestors came from. Do you ever feel a pull toward it? Write a short poem expressing your feelings.

To some people, a name is a private, almost secret affair. Do you have a secret name for yourself—a name known only to you?

How a Girl Got Her Chinese Name _____

Nellie Wong

On the first day of school the teacher asked me:
What do your parents call you at home?

I answered: Nellie.

Nellie? Nellie?
The teacher stressed the l's, whinnying like a horse.
No such name in Chinese for a name like Nellie.
We shall call you *Nah Lei*
which means *Where* or *Which Place*.

The teacher brushed my new name,
black on beige paper.
I practiced writing *Nah Lei*
holding the brush straight, dipping
the ink over and over.

After school I ran home.
Papa, Mama, the teacher says my name is *Nah Lei*.
I did not look my parents in the eye.

Nah Lei? Where? Which Place?
No, that will not do, my parents answered.
We shall give you a Chinese name,
we shall call you *Lai Oy*.

So back to school I ran,
announcing to my teacher and friends
that my name was no longer *Nah Lei,*
not *Where,* not *Which Place,*
but *Lai Oy, Beautiful Love,*
my own Chinese name.
I giggled as I thought:
Lai Oy could also mean *lost pocket*
depending on the heart
of a conversation.

But now in Chinese school
I was *Lai Oy,* to pull out of my pocket
every day, after American school,
even Saturday mornings,
from Nellie, from *Where,* from *Which Place*
to *Lai Oy,* to *Beautiful Love.*

Between these names
I never knew I would ever get lost.

RESPONDING

1. (a) How did the poet get her first Chinese name?
   (b) What does this name mean?

2. (a) Why did her parents give her a different Chinese
   name? (b) What does this name mean?

3. How do these names make her feel?

WRITING

Think about the *theme,* or central meaning, of this
poem. Then write a paragraph analyzing the theme.

A friend may well be reckoned the masterpiece of nature.

Ralph Waldo Emerson

Reaching Out

What value do you place on friendship?

Oath of Friendship _____

Anonymous, China, 1st Century B.C.
Translated by Arthur Waley

Shang ya!
I want to be your friend
For ever and ever without break or decay.
When the hills are all flat
And the rivers are all dry,
When it lightens and thunders in winter,
When it rains and snows in summer,
When Heaven and Earth mingle —
Not till then will I part from you.

RESPONDING

1. What does the poet want?

2. *Overstatement* is a form of exaggeration, of making
   things greater than they are. According to the poet,
   what five impossible things will happen before the
   two friends part?

WRITING

Write your own oath of friendship. Include in it at least
five impossible things that must happen before you and
your friend part.

Do you really know the people you pass in the street every day?

Sing a Song of People

Lois Lenski

Sing a song of people
  Walking fast or slow;
People in the city,
  Up and down they go.
    People on the sidewalk,
    People on the bus;
    People passing, passing,
    In back and front of us.
    People on the subway
    Underneath the ground;
    People riding taxis
    Round and round and round.
    People with their hats on,
    Going in the doors;
    People with umbrellas
    When it rains and pours.
People in tall buildings
And in stores below;
Riding elevators
Up and down they go.
People walking singly,
People in a crowd;
People saying nothing,
People talking loud.
People laughing, smiling,
Grumpy people too;
People who just hurry
And never look at you!

Sing a song of people
  Who like to come and go;
Sing of city people
  You see but never know!

RESPONDING

1. Where are the people whom the poet describes living?

2. These people are always in a hurry, always coming and going. What effect does this movement have on the poet's relationships with them?

WRITING

Read the poem aloud. Notice that it has a very definite *rhythm,* or pattern of stressed and unstressed syllables. Write a paragraph explaining how the rhythm of the poem helps create an image of people on the move.

Have you ever wanted to impress someone?

The Hero _____

Robert Graves

Slowly with bleeding nose and aching wrists
After tremendous use of feet and fists
He rises from the dusty schoolroom floor
And limps for solace to the girl next door
Boasting of kicks and punches, cheers and noise.
And far worse damage done to bigger boys.

RESPONDING

1. What has happened to the boy?

2. Why does he go for solace, or comfort, to the girl next door?

3. How does he try to impress her?

WRITING

What is a hero? Think about the boy in this poem. Can you describe him as a hero? Why or why not? Write a paragraph explaining your answer.

Can a friend make even the grayest of days seem blue?

Together _____

Paul Engle

Because we do
All things together
All things improve,
Even weather.

Our daily meat
And bread taste better,
Trees greener,
Rain is wetter.

Valentine _____

Donald Hall

Chipmunks jump, and
Greensnakes slither.
Rather burst than
Not be with her.

Bluebirds fight, but
Bears are stronger.
We've got fifty
Years or longer.

Hoptoads hop, but
Hogs are fatter.
Nothing else but
Us can matter.

My Valentine _____

Robert Louis Stevenson

I will make you brooches
And toys for your delight
Of bird song at morning
And starshine at night.
I will build a palace
Fit for you and me,

  Of green days in forests
  And blue days at sea.

RESPONDING

1. In the first poem, which details tell you that the
   speaker really enjoys the companionship of his friend?

2. In the second poem, why is the speaker filled with
   joy?

3. Love is often a relationship filled with magic. In the
   third poem, how will the speaker give magic back to
   his beloved?

WRITING

Each of these poems can be considered a valentine, or
token of love. Write a valentine to someone you cherish.

Have you ever wanted to scribble the name of your love across the sky?

Sunday

James Schuyler

The mint bed is in
bloom: lavender haze
day. The grass is
more than green and
throws up sharp and
cutting lights to
slice through the
plane tree leaves. And
on the cloudless blue
I scribble your name.

A Birthday

Christina Rossetti

My heart is like a singing bird
  Whose nest is in a watered shoot;
My heart is like an apple-tree
  Whose boughs are bent with thick-set fruit;
My heart is like a rainbow shell
  That paddles in a halcyon sea;
My heart is gladder than all these,
  Because my love is come to me.

Raise me a dais of silk and down;
   Hang it with vair and purple dyes;
Carve it in doves and pomegranates,
   And peacocks with a hundred eyes;
Work it in gold and silver grapes,
   In leaves and silver fleurs-de-lys;
Because the birthday of my life
   Is come, my love is come to me.

RESPONDING

1. Which details in "Sunday" create the impression of a perfect day?

2. What does the speaker do to make his perfect day complete?

3. In "A Birthday," the speaker uses three similes to describe the gladness in her heart. In what way is her heart like a singing bird?

4. In what way is the speaker's heart like an apple tree?

5. In what way is the speaker's heart like a rainbow shell?

6. Why does the poet title her poem "A Birthday"?

WRITING

Mood is the impression created by a poem or the feelings it arouses. Choose either "Surprise" or "A Birthday." Then write a paragraph analyzing the mood of this poem. Be sure to include the specific details that help create this mood.

49

Have you ever sat by the phone waiting for it to ring?

The Invention of the Telephone _____

Peter Klappert

The time it took he could have
crawled—on the hairs of his knuckles,
on his eyelids, on his teeth.

He could have chewed his way.
In a place without friction
he could have re-invented the wheel.

But he wanted you to be
proud of him, so he invented
the telephone before he called.

RESPONDING

1. *Exaggeration* is a form of figurative language. The
   speaker uses exaggeration to describe how long it took
   the person to call. What five things could this person
   have done before he called?

2. (a) What did the person do before he called? (b) Do
   you think the speaker wants you to take these words
   literally—that is, at face value, or do they have a
   figurative meaning? If they do, what is it?

WRITING

Figurative language consists of words and phrases not
meant to be taken literally—that is, at face value.
Discuss the use of figurative language in this poem.
Then write a paragraph analyzing its use.

Have you ever felt absolutely alone?

If You Have Had Your Midnights

Mari Evans

if you have had
your midnights
and they have drenched
your barren guts
with tears

I sing you sunrise
and love
and someone to touch

RESPONDING

1. Think of how you feel when you sit awake at
   midnight, unable to sleep. What do you think the
   speaker means by the term "your midnights"?

2. With what will the speaker replace your midnights?

WRITING

A *metaphor* is a figurative comparison between two
basically unlike things that does not use the word *like* or
as. For example, if we wanted to suggest that someone
was sleeping lightly, we might use a metaphor comparing
his sleeping to the way a cat sleeps: *He is merely
catnapping.* Reread "If You Have Had Your Midnights."
Then write a paragraph analyzing the use of metaphor in
it.

How great is love?

love is more thicker than forget

e. e. cummings

love is more thicker than forget
more thinner than recall
more seldom than a wave is wet
more frequent than to fail

it is most mad and moonly
and less it shall unbe
than all the sea which only
is deeper than the sea

love is less always than to win
less never than alive
less bigger than the least begin
less littler than forgive

it is most sane and sunly
and more it cannot die
than all the sky which only
is higher than the sky

RESPONDING

(a) Which simile tells you that love does not come
frequently? (b) Which simile tells you that it is lasting?

WRITING

Write your own similes describing the power of love.
Select the most effective ones and turn them into a poem.

Has *another person's smile or laugh ever filled your heart with joy?*

After the Rain

Paul B. Janeczko

Your smile,
with the spectacular softness
of a rainbow,
makes me
laugh and wish I were
the sky.

When You Laugh

Ingrid Jonker

Your laughter is like a burst pomegranate
Laugh again
so I can hear how pomegranates laugh

RESPONDING

1. (a) In the first poem, to what does the speaker compare the person's smile? (b) Why does he wish he were the sky?

2. In the second poem, why does the speaker compare the person's laughter to a pomegranate?

WRITING

Think of someone whose smile or laughter fills you with joy. Using a simile, write a three-line poem describing this person.

Will you still love when you grow old?

Jenny Kiss'd Me

Leigh Hunt

Jenny kiss'd me when we met,
  Jumping from the chair she sat in:
Time, you thief, who love to get
  Sweets into your list, put that in!
Say I'm weary, say I'm sad,
  Say that health and wealth have miss'd me,
Say I'm growing old, but add,
  Jenny kiss'd me.

RESPONDING

1. *Personification* means giving human qualities to inanimate objects or abstract ideas. In the poem, how does the speaker personify time?

2. What solace, or comfort, will the speaker have in his old age?

WRITING

Imagine you have grown old. Write a poem telling what remembrances of love will fill you with joy.

Can a person's love bring security?

Senses of Insecurity _____

Maya Angelou

I couldn't tell fact from fiction
  or if my dream was true,
The only sure prediction
  in this whole world was you.
I'd touched your features inchly
  heard love and dared the cost.
The scented spiel reeled me unreal
  and found my senses lost.

RESPONDING

1. What one thing in the whole world does the speaker consider sure?

2. Reread the last two lines of this poem. (a) *Paraphrase* them; that is, put them in your own words. (b) In light of the meaning of these two lines, explain the title.

WRITING

Read this poem aloud. Listen carefully to its rhythm and its use of rhyme. Then write a paragraph analyzing the rhythm and rhyme scheme of the poem.

Does loneliness cause us to reach out to others?

Pocket Poem _____

Ted Kooser

If this comes creased and creased again and soiled
as if I'd opened it a thousand times
to see if what I'd written here was right,
it's all because I looked for you too long
to put it in your pocket. Midnight says
the little gifts of loneliness come wrapped
by nervous fingers. What I wanted this
to say was that I want to be so close
that when you find it, it is warm from me.

RESPONDING

1. Why might the poem be creased and soiled?

2. (a) What are "the little gifts of loneliness"? (b) Why do they come "wrapped by nervous fingers"?

3. What does the poet want his poem to say?

WRITING

This poem is written as though it were a note. Think about someone to whom you would like to send a pocket poem. Then write a short pocket poem expressing your feelings.

Can love come when it is least expected?

On Being Introduced to You

Eve Merriam

No watch
can tell love's time:
the hour is always
unbidden, when least expected,
as now.

Joy comes
as a light craft
darting on the surface
of the sea, then dropping anchor
to stay.

Cinquains:
five lines, unrhymed;
start with two syllables,
go to four, six, eight, but at length
just two.

RESPONDING

1. (a) What is "love's time"? (b) When does love come?

2. How is love like a light craft?

WRITING

A *cinquain* contains five unrhymed lines. Write a
cinquain about your first meeting with someone who
turned out to be very important to you. Your first line
should have two syllables; your second, four; your third,
six; your fourth, eight; and your last line, two.

Can a swimming lesson be a lesson in living?

First Lesson _____

Philip Booth

Lie back, daughter, let your head
be tipped back in the cup of my hand.
Gently, and I will hold you. Spread
your arms wide, lie out on the stream
and look high at the gulls. A dead-
man's-float is face down. You will dive
and swim soon enough where this tidewater
ebbs to the sea. Daughter, believe
me, when you tire on the long thrash
to your island, lie up, and survive.
As you float now, where I held you
and let go, remember when fear
cramps your heart what I told you:
lie gently and wide to the light-year
stars, lie back, and the sea will hold you.

RESPONDING

1. At face value, this poem is about a swimming lesson.
   What does the father tell his daughter to do instead of
   a dead man's float?

2. The father wants to teach his daughter to survive in
   the water. What else does he want to teach her?

WRITING

Theme is the central meaning of a poem. Think about
what the father wants his daughter to learn. Then write a
paragraph analyzing the theme of the poem.

Do we die many little deaths before our end?

Little Elegy
for a child who
skipped rope

X. J. Kennedy

Here lies resting, out of breath,
Out of turns, Elizabeth
Whose quicksilver toes not quite
Cleared the whirring edge of night.

Earth whose circles round us skim
Till they catch the lightest limb,
Shelter now Elizabeth
And for her sake trip up death.

RESPONDING

1. Although her toes are quicksilver fast, even Elizabeth cannot help but be tripped up by the rope. What metaphor does the poet use to describe this rope?

2. An elegy is a poem of mourning. (a) Why does the poet compose a "little elegy" for Elizabeth? (b) What does he wish could happen?

WRITING

"Little Elegy" gains its power through figurative language. Write a paragraph analyzing the effect of the use of figurative language on this poem.

What legacies have enriched your life?

Legacies _____

her grandmother called her from the playground
    "yes, ma'am"
    "i want chu to learn how to make rolls" said the old
woman proudly
but the little girl didn't want
to learn how because she knew
even if she couldn't say it that
that would mean when the old one died she would be
        less
dependent on her spirit so
she said
    "i don't want to know how to make no rolls"
with her lips poked out
and the old woman wiped her hands on
her apron saying "lord
    these children"
and neither of them ever
said what they meant
and i guess nobody ever does

RESPONDING

Why do people have trouble saying what they mean to
those they love?

WRITING

List all the legacies, or gifts, you would pass on to your
future children. Select one of them. Then write a poem
bequeathing, or passing on, your legacy.

What gift would you make for the world?

The Harp

Bruce Weigl

When he was my age and I was already a boy
my father made a machine in the garage.
A wired piece of steel
with many small and beautiful welds
ground so smooth they resembled rows of pearls.

He went broke with whatever it was.
He held it so carefully in his arms.
He carried it foundry to foundry.
I think it was his harp.

I think it was what he longed to make
with his hands for the world.

He moved it finally from the locked closet
to the bedroom
to the garage again
where he hung it on the wall
until I climbed and pulled it down
and rubbed it clean
and tried to make it work.

RESPONDING

1. What is the father's gift to the world?

2. Why does the son retrieve it from the garage?

3. A *symbol* is an object that represents something else. For example, a red rose is often considered a symbol for love, and a mirror a symbol for vanity. In this poem, what does the harp represent?

WRITING

"Legacy" and "The Harp" are both about gifts from the past. Write a paragraph comparing and contrasting the two poems.

Why do people love attics?

Herbs in the Attic _____

Marilyn Waniek

A cat by the fireside, purring.
But I don't stop there; I go
through the living room and up the stairs.
My little brother stirs in his crib.
My sister and I sleep in our tumbled rooms,
and our parents sleep together,
fingers intertwined.

The second stairway's narrow.
It darkens when I close the door
behind me. And I climb up to the attic,
to the bustles and pantaloons
hidden in trunks, the diaries and love-letters,
the photographs, the rings,
the envelopes full of hair.

Here's the old silverware
Great Aunt Irene and Uncle Eric used.
Her fork is curved
from her life-long habit
of scraping the plate.
His knife is broader,
the better for buttering bread.

Here are the bookcases of discarded books:
Tarzan, Zane Grey, a textbook Shakespeare,
piles of *National Geographic, Look* and *Life:*
enough to last me a while.

I sit on the dusty floor
and open a book.
Dream music fills the air
like the scent of dried herbs.

RESPONDING

1. The girl leaves the comfort of the present to go up to the attic. (a) What does she find there? (b) What do these things *symbolize*, or represent?

2. Reread the last two lines of the poem. (a) What is the dream music that fills the air? (b) Why is dried herbs a fitting metaphor for treasures from the past?

WRITING

Write a paragraph analyzing the use of symbols in "Herbs in the Attic." In your paragraph, be sure to pay particular attention to the title.

Surprise is the greatest gift which life can grant us.

Boris Pasternak

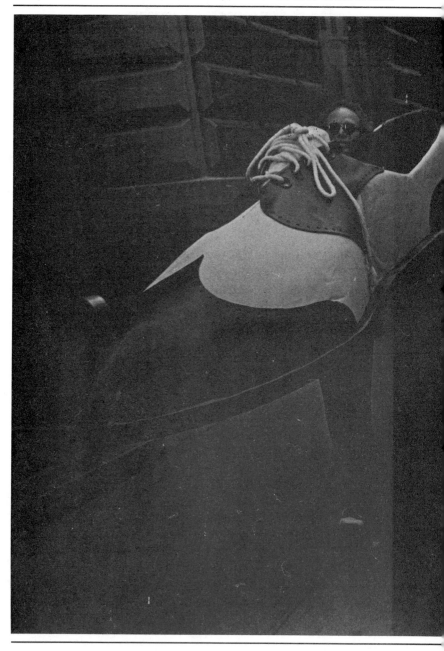

Sudden
Surprises

What surprise is in store for Melissa?

Fancy Dive _____

Shel Silverstein

The fanciest dive that ever was dove
Was done by Melissa of Coconut Grove
She bounced on the board and flew in the air
With a twist of her head and a twirl of her hair
She did thirty-four jackknives, backflipped and spun,
Quadruple gainered and reached for the sun
And then somersaulted nine times and a quarter
And looked down and saw that the pool had no water.

RESPONDING

1. The first seven lines in this poem build up your expectations. At first, what do you think this poem will tell you about Melissa's fancy dive?

2. The poem takes an unexpected turn in the last line. What fact ruins Melissa's dive?

3. What effect does this sudden change have on the poem? In other words, how does it make you respond?

WRITING

Try writing your own eight-line poem with a sudden change of direction. Start by describing a simple action or event. With each line, build up your readers' expectations by piling up the details. Then make the last line come as a surprise.

Does a blue day call for emergency action?

Blue Alert

Eve Merriam

Quick!

Empty the offices
rush all the lecture halls
abandon the copy machines
burst out

EMERGEN—

see the sky
unboxed
lid off
shaking loose

What number do we call to
bring it down
box it
back in?

RESPONDING

(a) Why do the people want to box the sky back in?
(b) Why is it fitting that they respond to a blue day in
this way?

WRITING

Imagine that a rainbow alert were suddenly called in
your school. First brainstorm with your classmates to
develop a list of things students might do. Then write a
poem describing the experience.

What surprise is in store for the waking sunbather?

Waking from a Nap on the Beach

May Swenson

Sounds like big
rashers of bacon frying.
I look up from where I'm lying
expecting to see stripes

red and white. My eyes drop shut,
stunned by the sun.
Now the foam is flame, the long
troughs charcoal, but

still it chuckles and sizzles, it
burns and burns, it never gets done.
The sea is that
fat.

RESPONDING

1. (a) What does the sunbather think she hears when she wakes up? (b) What does she really hear?

2. (a) To what does the sunbather compare the foam? (b) To what does she compare the troughs?

3. What really has been burning all day in the sun?

WRITING

Write a short paragraph analyzing the use of similes and metaphors in this poem.

Does the taste of the first salad of March come as a startling surprise?

The First Salad of March ____

Marge Piercy

Thinnings of the rows,
Chinese cabbage, lettuce, sorrel,
cress; nipped ends of herbs
returning, mint and thyme;
violet leaves poking up
in clusters like armies
of teddy bears emerging
ears first from the earth;
the Egyptian onions that multiply
underground; the spears
of garlic shoots. The mixture
huddles, skimpy in the bowl.

The salad explodes in the mouth,
green romancandles.
It is succulent, dainty,
intense. It is crisp
as new money.
It lights up my blood
and urges fur from
the backs of my hands.
I want to roll in leaves
that are still lumps
on twigs. First salad
strong and fierce and plaintive:
love at age five. Spring
makes new the taste of lettuce
fresh as a tear.

RESPONDING

1. The poet describes a five-year-old girl eating the first
   salad of March. To help you experience eating the
   salad for yourself, the poet uses many *sensory
   details*—details appealing to the senses. For example,
   the details *Chinese cabbage, lettuce, sorrel,* and *cress*
   appeal to your sense of taste. Which other sensory
   details appeal to your sense of taste?

2. To make you realize how fresh this salad is, the poet
   makes the individual ingredients seem alive. (a) What
   simile does she use to make the violet leaves come
   alive? (b) Do you think this simile is effective? Why or
   why not?

3. When mixed in the bowl, the salad seems skimpy.
   What happens when it enters the mouth?

4. This first salad is so fresh that by eating it the young
   girl feels at one with nature. What *image*, or word
   picture, creates this feeling of closeness to the natural
   world?

5. In what way is the taste of lettuce as "fresh as a tear"?

WRITING

Some people feel that taste is our most vivid of senses.
Select something you enjoy eating. List as many details
appealing to your sense of taste as you can. Then write a
poem describing eating this object, using as many
sensory details as you can.

Have you bitten into a strawberry and been surprised by its sweetness?

Strawberries

Judith Hemschemeyer

The first time I went to the fields alone
I didn't see the strawberries until
I tripped and fell and lay completely still.
Then they came out. One by one at first,
Then clumped in constellations they emerged,
A galaxy of trembling, rooted stars.

But when I picked one and brought it back to earth,
My breathing on it moved like a wind,
And it turned over in my giant hand
So sure of what it was that it could
Seem to be the accidental meeting
Of three glowing, polished drops of blood.

Berry, berries crushed against my tongue,
Broke the seal on a longing for sweetness
I didn't know was hidden in me.
I ate, reached out and ate. Chords of scent rose
From green, folded hay, my rolling body
And the red stains ripening on my clothes.

I whispered secrets to myself. I felt
The earth tip and the afternoon slide
Toward the edge as I stood up. So I ran
To the dark, inside place called home to bless
Beds and tables with my sweet, red hands.
But they told me I had ruined my dress.

RESPONDING

1. The speaker in this poem is a young girl. (a) When does she first see the strawberries? (b) In the first stanza, what *metaphor*, or comparison, does she use to describe them?

2. *Personification* means giving human qualities to inanimate objects or abstract ideas. How does the girl personify the strawberries?

3. (a) What surprise does the girl find when she crushes the strawberries against her tongue? (b) How does the taste of strawberries make her feel? Find details to support your answer.

4. Why does the girl want to touch everything with her red hands?

5. (a) To whom does the *they* in this poem refer? (b) How do *they* react to her actions?

WRITING

Write a paragraph comparing and contrasting the girl's reaction with the reaction of the "they" in this poem. In your paragraph, explore the way in which the contrast between these two reactions reveals the *theme*, or deeper meaning of the poem.

Have you ever found yourself in a ridiculous situation?

The Bagel

David Ignatow

I stopped to pick up the bagel
rolling away in the wind,
annoyed with myself
for having dropped it
as it were a portent.
Faster and faster it rolled,
with me running after it
bent low, gritting my teeth,
and I found myself doubled over
and rolling down the street
head over heels, one complete somersault
after another like a bagel
and strangely happy with myself.

RESPONDING

1. A *portent* is an omen, a sign of something significant about to happen. At first, do you think the speaker considers his dropping the bagel as a portent of good or bad things about to occur? Why?

2. In what way does the dropping of the bagel prove to be a portent after all?

WRITING

We have all had things happen to us that at first we thought were bad but that turned out to be good. Think about such an event. Discuss it with your classmates. Then write a short poem describing the situation.

Do people always behave the way you expect them to?

Lord Cray

Edward Gorey

The sight of his guests filled Lord Cray
At breakfast with horrid dismay,
  So he launched off the spoons
  The pits from his prunes
At their heads as they neared the buffet.

RESPONDING

1. What is surprising about Lord Cray's behavior?

2. Why does the way he acts fill us, the readers, with secret pleasure?

WRITING

"Lord Cray" is a good example of a *limerick*. This form of humorous poetry has five lines. The first, second, and fifth lines follow the same rhythmic pattern and the words at the end of these lines rhyme. The third and fourth lines follow their own rhythmic pattern and the words at the end of these lines rhyme.

Have a limerick contest with your classmates. Each student should write two or three and read them aloud. Then select the ten best limericks and publish them in booklet form.

Have you ever wondered if a ride on a roller-coaster
would go on forever?

Flight of the Roller-Coaster —
Raymond Souster

Once more around should do it, the man confided . . .

And sure enough, when the roller-coaster reached the
    peak
Of the giant curve above me—screech of its wheels
Almost drowned by the shriller cries of the riders—

Inside of the dip and plunge with its landslide of screams
It rose in the air like a movieland magic carpet, some
    wonderful bird,
And without fuss or fanfare swooped slowly across the
    amusement park,
Over Spook's Castle, ice-cream booths, shooting-gallery:
    and losing no height

Made the last yards above the beach, where the
    cucumber-cool
Brakeman in the last seat saluted
A lady about to change from her bathing-suit.

Then, as many witnesses duly reported, headed leisurely
    over the water,
Disappearing mysteriously all too soon behind a low-lying
    flight of clouds.

RESPONDING

1. At the start of the poem, the man says, "Once more around should do it." In light of what happens, what does his statement mean?

2. When does the roller-coaster disappear?

3. *Tone* is the attitude expressed by the poem. How does the poet create a matter-of-fact tone in this poem?

WRITING

This poem is based on something we all *suspect* could happen but *know* could not happen. Brainstorm with your classmates to create a list of incredible events. Then select one of these events. Using a matter-of-fact tone, write a poem describing it.

What surprise does Little Red Riding Hood have in store for the wolf?

Little Red Riding Hood and the Wolf

Roald Dahl

As soon as Wolf began to feel
That he would like a decent meal,
He went and knocked on Grandma's door.
When Grandma opened it, she saw
The sharp white teeth, the horrid grin,
And Wolfie said, "May I come in?"
Poor Grandmamma was terrified,
"He's going to eat me up!" she cried.
And she was absolutely right.
He ate her up in one big bite.
But Grandmamma was small and tough,
And Wolfie wailed, "That's not enough!
I haven't yet begun to feel
That I have had a decent meal!"
He ran around the kitchen yelping,
"I've *got* to have a second helping!"
Then added with a frightful leer,
"I'm therefore going to wait right here
Till Little Miss Red Riding Hood
Comes home from walking in the wood."
He quickly put on Grandma's clothes,
(Of course he hadn't eaten those).
He dressed himself in coat and hat.
He put on shoes and after that
He even brushed and curled his hair,
Then sat himself in Grandma's chair.
In came the little girl in red.
She stopped. She stared. And then she said,

"What great big ears you have, Grandma."
"All the better to hear you with," the Wolf replied.
"What great big eyes you have, Grandma,"
said Little Red Riding Hood.
"All the better to see you with," the Wolf replied.

He sat there watching her and smiled.
He thought, I'm going to eat this child.
Compared with her old Grandmamma
She's going to taste like caviar.
Then Little Red Riding Hood said, *"But Grandma,*
what a lovely great big furry coat you have on."

"That's wrong!" cried Wolf. "Have you forgot
To tell me what BIG TEETH I've got?
Ah well, no matter what you say,
I'm going to eat you anyway."
The small girl smiles. One eyelid flickers.
She whips a pistol from her knickers.
She aims it at the creature's head
And *bang bang bang*, she shoots him dead.
A few weeks later, in the wood,
I came across Miss Riding Hood.
But what a change! No cloak of red,
No silly hood upon her head.
She said, "Hello, and do please note
My lovely furry wolfskin coat."

RESPONDING

A *narrative poem* tells a story. (a) What story does this
poem retell? (b) How would you describe the tone?

WRITING

Select a familiar fairy tale. Then write a poem retelling
it. Use the same tone as Roald Dahl uses in his poem.

Have you ever seen a television announcer with poor teeth?

Reflections Dental

Phyllis McGinley

How pure, how beautiful, how fine
Do teeth on television shine!
No flutist flutes, no dancer twirls,
But comes equipped with matching pearls.
Gleeful announcers all are born
With sets like rows of hybrid corn.
Clowns, critics, clergy, commentators,
Ventriloquists and roller skaters,
M.C.s who beat their palms together,
The girl who diagrams the weather,
The crooner crooning for his supper—
All flash white treasures, lower and upper.
With miles of smiles the airwaves teem,
And each an orthodontist's dream.

'Twould please my eye as gold a miser's—
One charmer with uncapped incisors.

RESPONDING

1. In the first fourteen lines the poet describes a specific situation. What does she describe?

2. Why do the last two lines come as a surprise?

WRITING

Write a paragraph explaining the tone of this poem. Pay attention to how the poet sets up this situation.

Can telephone poles fall in love?

Simultaneously _____

David Ignatow

Simultaneously, five thousand miles apart,
two telephone poles, shaking and roaring
and hissing gas, rose from their emplacements
straight up, leveled off and headed
for each other's land, alerted radar
and ground defense, passed each other
in midair, escorted by worried planes,
and plunged into each other's place,
steaming and silent and standing straight,
sprouting leaves.

RESPONDING

1. What amazing event happens in this poem?

2. *Personification* means giving human qualities to
   inanimate objects. (a) In what way do the telephone
   poles act like eager lovers? (b) Why is it fitting that
   the telephone poles sprout leaves?

WRITING

Select one of the following objects or choose one of your
own: a fishing pole, a tooth brush, a lamp, a house.
Imagine it were to come alive. Write a short poem
describing what it would do.

What surprise is in store for us when winter turns to spring?

April 5, 1974 _____

Richard Wilbur

The air was soft, the ground still cold.
In the dull pasture where I strolled
Was something I could not believe.
Dead grass appeared to slide and heave,
Though still too frozen-flat to stir,
And rocks to twitch, and all to blur.
What was this rippling of the land?
Was matter getting out of hand
And making free with natural law?
I stopped and blinked, and then I saw
A fact as eerie as a dream.
There was a subtle flood of steam
Moving upon the face of things.
It came from standing pools and springs
And what of snow was still around;
It came of winter's giving ground
So that the freeze was coming out,
As when a set mind, blessed by doubt,
Relaxes into mother-wit.
Flowers, I said, will come of it.

RESPONDING

1. What is causing the rippling of the land?

2. According to the speaker, what will be the result of this change?

WRITING

The changing of the seasons has captured the imagination of many a poet. Write your own poem describing this event.

Have you noticed that mushrooms seem to appear overnight?

Mushrooms ⎯⎯⎯⎯⎯⎯⎯⎯⎯⎯⎯

Sylvia Plath

Overnight, very
Whitely, discreetly,
Very quietly

Our toes, our noses
Take hold on the loam,
Acquire the air.

Nobody sees us,
Stops us, betrays us;
The small grains make room.

Soft fists insist on
Heaving the needles,
The leafy bedding,

Even the paving.
Our hammers, our rams,
Earless and eyeless,

Perfectly voiceless,
Widen the crannies,
Shoulder through holes. We

Diet on water,
On crumbs of shadow,
Bland-mannered, asking

Little or nothing.
So many of us!
So many of us!

We are shelves, we are
Tables, we are meek,
We are edible,

Nudgers and shovers
In spite of ourselves
Our kind multiplies:

We shall by morning
Inherit the earth.
Our foot's in the door.

RESPONDING

1. Who is the speaker in this poem?

2. The poet creates a picture of the mushrooms as a silent army. Which details help create this picture?

3. What do the mushrooms plan to do?

4. What is the meaning of the last line?

WRITING

Discuss the *mood*, or feeling, of this poem. Then write a paragraph explaining the way in which the poet uses personification to create a mood of menace.

Are mushrooms really sorcerers spreading death?

Mushrooms

Mary Oliver

Rain, and then
the cool pursed
lips of the wind
draw them
out of the ground—
red and yellow skulls
pummeling upward
through leaves,
through grasses,
through sand; astonishing
in their suddenness,
their quietude,
their wetness, they appear
on fall mornings, some
balancing in the earth
on one hoof
packed with poison,
others billowing
chunkily, and delicious—
those who know
walk out to gather, choosing
the benign from flocks
of glitterers, sorcerers,
russulas,
panther caps
shark-white death angels
in their torn veils
looking innocent as sugar
but full of paralysis:

to eat
is to stagger down
fast as mushrooms themselves
when they are done being perfect
and overnight
slide back under the shining
fields of rain.

RESPONDING

1. Words have both *denotations* and *connotations*. The *denotation* of a word is its dictionary meaning. The *connotation* consists of the feelings and thoughts it stirs up in the reader. (a) What feelings and thoughts are stirred up by the word *death*? (b) Why do you think the poet chose to describe the mushrooms as skulls rather than as buttons?

2. (a) What nouns does the poet use to further this *image*, or picture, of the mushrooms? (b) How does her choice of metaphors make this image stronger?

3. In what way are the mushrooms perfect?

WRITING

Write a paragraph comparing and contrasting Sylvia Plath's poem "Mushrooms" with Mary Oliver's.

Do you ever surprise even yourself?

Geometry

Rita Dove

I prove a theorem and the house expands:
the windows jerk free to hover near the ceiling,
the ceiling floats away with a sigh.

As the walls clear themselves of everything
but transparency, the scent of carnations
leaves with them. I am out in the open

and above the windows have hinged into butterflies,
sunlight glinting where they've intersected.
They are going to some point true and unproven.

RESPONDING

1. The speaker is so amazed by her proving a theorem
   that the house seems to expand. (a) What happens to
   the windows? (b) What happens to the ceiling?

2. Soon the speaker finds herself out in the open. What
   does she see above her?

3. Think about geometry. What is the point "true and
   unproven" to which the butterflies are going?

WRITING

Think about a difficult school subject. Write a poem
expressing how you feel when you do well in it. You
might choose to begin in one of the following ways: (1) I
solve an algebraic equation and . . . . (2) I diagram a
sentence and . . . . (3) I perform a lab experiment and . . . .

Have you ever read a book you couldn't put down?

Books Fall Open

David McCord

Books fall open,
you fall in,
delighted where
you've never been;
hear voices not once
heard before,
reach world on world
through door on door;
find unexpected
keys to things
locked up beyond
imaginings.
What *might* you be,
perhaps *become*,
because one book
is somewhere? Some
wise delver into
wisdom, wit,
and wherewithal
has written it.
True books will venture,
dare you out,
whisper secrets,
maybe shout
across the gloom
to you in need,
who hanker for
a book to read.

RESPONDING

1. According to the poem, what could you find in a book?

2. What will true books do?

WRITING

"Books Fall Open" is a *lyric poem* — a poem that expresses one's thoughts and feelings on a subject. It is the most musical of poetry, often following a regular pattern of sounds. Think about a subject about which you feel strongly. Then write a lyric poem expressing your feelings.

Be ahead of all farewells, as if they were behind you, like the winter that is just departing.

Rainer Maria Rilke

Saying Good-Bye

Does your life need some housecleaning?

Housecleaning

Nikki Giovanni

i always liked housecleaning
even as a child
i dug straightening
the cabinets
putting new paper on
the shelves
washing the refrigerator
inside out
and unfortunately this habit has
carried over and i find
i must remove you
from my life

RESPONDING

1. Many people find housecleaning an unwelcome task.
   How does the speaker feel about housecleaning?

2. The purpose of housecleaning is to clean up or bring
   order to the house. To what does the speaker want to
   bring order now?

WRITING

We think of saying good-bye as a sad event, but the
speaker in this poem makes of it a positive experience.
Write a short poem saying good-bye to something you
would like to leave behind or get rid of. For example,
perhaps you are taking a course you find difficult. You
might write a poem saying good-bye to algebra.

Can the departure of a friend make even an ice-cream cone taste like prunes?

Since Hanna Moved Away

Judith Viorst

The tires on my bike are flat.
The sky is grouchy gray.
At least it sure feels like that
Since Hanna moved away.

Chocolate ice cream tastes like prunes.
December's come to stay.
They've taken back the Mays and Junes
Since Hanna moved away.

Flowers smell like halibut.
Velvet feels like hay.
Every handsome dog's a mutt
Since Hanna moved away.

Nothing's fun to laugh about.
Nothing's fun to play.
They call me, but I won't come out
Since Hanna moved away.

RESPONDING

Which changes in the speaker's behavior suggest that she is saddened by Hanna's departure?

WRITING

Think about what a special person's departure meant to you. Then write a short poem telling how your world changed when this person went away.

Does separation bring pain?

Separation
W. S. Merwin

Your absence has gone through me
Like thread through a needle.
Everything I do is stitched with its color.

Separation
P. Wolny

Each day
ungently leads
into the night:
a rose unopened,
blackened by the cold.

RESPONDING

1. In the first poem, the poet uses a simile to describe the pain of absence. What is this simile?

2. What metaphor does the poet then use to describe how widespread the pain caused by the absence is?

3. In the second poem, what adverb describes how day leads into night? Why is this word particularly effective?

4. (a) What metaphor in this poem describes separation?
   (b) What is the meaning of this metaphor?

WRITING

W. S. Merwin and P. Wolny both wrote about the same topic. Write a paragraph comparing and contrasting their use of figurative language—similes and metaphors.

What can you say about a friend who went away?

Poem

Langston Hughes

I loved my friend.
He went away from me.
There's nothing more to say.
The poem ends,
Soft as it began—
I loved my friend.

The Opposite of Two

Richard Wilbur

What is the opposite of *two*?
A lonely me, a lonely you.

RESPONDING

1. In the first poem, what is the one thing the poet can say about his departed friend?

2. In the second poem, what is the opposite of two?

WRITING

Write a two-line poem telling your own definition of the opposite of two.

Do the words "good-bye" carry their own sound?

The Departure

Frank Steele

When you go away
you become everything I believe
you are, the steady light
from the lamps, warm
from a distance on my skin,
the piano still playing
somewhere in my mind, curtains
blowing at the window
speaking to me.

RESPONDING

1. What does the beloved become after she departs?

2. What details create the image of warmth and beauty?

WRITING

In "The Departures," the poet uses metaphors to create
the impression of the beloved. Using metaphors, write a
short poem saying good-bye to someone.

Can sadness rise from the floor of the heart?

Goodbye

Sherod Santos

The great sun has changed itself into a pumpkin moon.
The highways glide out of an ocean of air
Like children's slides out of backyard pools.
And the filtered smokestacks give off fumes
Less visible than those which rise from the floor
Of the heart, though they burn all the same,
So the people outdoors appear all day
To be wiping a sad movie from their eyes—
A movie in which, for days to come, and whenever
Two people are seen parting on the street,
Some closing melody is replayed once more
While the one who is saying goodbye
Lets go the hand of the one left standing.

RESPONDING

1. Through the use of imagery, the poet creates a mood of sadness. Which image tells you that day has changed to night?

2. Even the air is grayed by the smokestacks giving off fumes. Where are the fumes even more visible?

3. Think about the last two lines. (a) Who is left with the greater sadness? (b) How do you know this?

WRITING

List images of sadness. Using the images you find most effective, write a short lyric poem.

Does love itself sometimes need a rest?

So, We'll Go No More A-Roving

Lord Byron

So, we'll go no more a-roving
  So late into the night,
Though the heart be still as loving,
  And the moon be still as bright.

For the sword outwears its sheath,
  And the soul wears out the breast,
And the heart must pause to breathe,
  And love itself have rest.

Though the night was made for loving,
  And the day returns too soon,
Yet we'll go no more a-roving
  By the light of the moon.

RESPONDING

1. (a) How can a sword wear out its sheath, or case?
   (b) How can the soul wear out the breast?

2. Why will the speaker go no more a-roving?

WRITING

"So, We'll Go No More A-Roving" is very musical. Write a paragraph examining its rhythmic structure.

Can love live on even after the beloved is gone?

Music, When Soft Voices Die

Percy Bysshe Shelley

Music, when soft voices die,
Vibrates in the memory—
Odours, when sweet violets sicken,
Live within the sense they quicken.

Rose leaves, when the rose is dead,
Are heap'd for the beloved's bed;
And so thy thoughts, when thou art gone,
Love itself shall slumber on.

RESPONDING

1. (a) How does music live on after it is over? (b) How do odors live on after the violets sicken and die?

2. How does love live on once the beloved is gone?

WRITING

This poem makes its point about love by telling how music and odors continue in the memory. Brainstorm with your classmates to list other items that live on in this way. Then write another stanza for this poem. In it, describe two of these objects.

Have you ever felt as if you were Miss Blues'es child?

Miss Blues'es Child

Langston Hughes

If the blues would let me,
Lord knows I would smile.
If the blues would let me,
I would smile, smile, smile.
Instead of that I'm cryin'—
I must be Miss Blues'es child.

You were my moon up in the sky,
At night my wishing star.
I love you, oh, I love you so—
But you have gone so far!

Now my days are lonely,
And night-time drives me wild.
In my heart I'm crying,
I'm just Miss Blues'es child!

RESPONDING

1. Why is the speaker crying?

2. Why does he feel that he is Miss Blues'es child?

WRITING

The blues is a style of jazz telling of sorrow and sadness.
Take time out to sing the blues. Write a short poem you
could use as a blues song. Then perform it for your
classmates.

What gift will you leave behind you?

No Labor-Savings Machine ___
Walt Whitman

No labor-savings machine,
Nor discovery have I made,
Nor will I be able to leave behind me any wealthy
   bequest to found a hospital or library,
Nor reminiscence of any deed of courage for America,
Nor literary success, nor intellect, nor book for the
   book-shelf,
But a few carols vibrating through the air I leave,
For comrades and lovers.

RESPONDING

1. What will the speaker not be able to leave behind him?

2. What will he leave behind him?

3. Which of these gifts do you think the speaker considers the greatest? Why?

WRITING

We all want to be remembered. Write a short poem telling how you will make your mark on the future.

What does it mean to be truly alone?

For Laurie

May Sarton

The people she loved are leaving
Her one by one
And she is left with the grieving,
Herself alone.

Herself who wakes in the morning
Now it is May
Like a small child mourning
A lost day.

Herself and the mountain near,
Ancient friend,
Herself in her ninetieth year
When lilacs bend

Under their weight of bloom
And ninety springs
Flow through her upstairs room,
And memory sings.

Alive to the loving past
She conjures her own.
Nothing is wholly lost —
Sun on the stone.

And lilacs in their splendor
Like lost friends
Come back through grief to tell her
Love never ends.

Acquainted with the Night___

Robert Frost

I have been one acquainted with the night.
I have walked out in rain—and back in rain.
I have outwalked the furthest city light.

I have looked down the saddest city lane.
I have passed by the watchman on his beat
And dropped my eyes, unwilling to explain.

I have stood still and stopped the sound of feet
When far away an interrupted cry
Came over houses from another street,

But not to call me back or say good-bye;
And further still at an unearthly height,
One luminary clock against the sky

Proclaimed the time was neither wrong nor right.
I have been one acquainted with the night.

RESPONDING

1. In the first poem, why is the woman grieving?

2. How does memory help her conquer her grief?

3. In the second poem, what does the speaker mean when he says that he has been "acquainted with the night"?

WRITING

Think about a time when you felt really lonely. Freewrite about the way you felt. Then, using the pronoun "I" to begin each line, write a two-stanza poem about your "acquaintance with the night."

How do geese know when it is time to depart?

Something Told the
Wild Geese

Rachel Field

Something told the wild geese
   It was time to go.
Though the fields lay golden
   Something whispered—"Snow."
Leaves were green and stirring,
   Berries, luster-glossed,
But beneath warm feathers
   Something cautioned—"Frost."
All the sagging orchards
   Steamed with amber spice,
But each wild breast stiffened
   At remembered ice.
Something told the wild geese
   It was time to fly—
Summer sun was on their wings,
   Winter in their cry.

Wild Goose

Curtis Heath

He climbs the wind above
  green clouds of pine,
Honking to hail the
  gathering migration,
And, arching toward the
  south, pulls to align
His flight into the great
  spearhead formation.

He'll find a bayou land of
  hidden pools,
And bask amid lush fern
  and water lily
Far from the frozen world
  of earth-bound fools
Who, shivering, maintain
  that geese are silly.

RESPONDING

1. In the first poem, what tells the geese to go?

2. In the second poem, what is the wild goose able to accomplish?

WRITING

One form of *irony* results from the difference between what appears to be true and what actually proves to be true. For example, imagine you have a stamp collection. In it, you have many stamps for which you have paid a lot of money. You also have one stamp that you think is worthless. You keep it, though, because a dear aunt gave it to you years ago. It would be ironic if this stamp proved to be the most valuable one in your collection.

In "Wild Goose," think about why the poet calls people fools. Discuss why the people call geese silly. Then write a paragraph explaining why the last stanza is ironic.

What is the most final of good-byes?

Little Things _____

James Stephens

Little things, that run, and quail,
And die, in silence and despair!

Little things, that fight, and fail,
And fall, on sea, and earth, and air!

All trapped and frightened little things,
The mouse, the coney, hear our prayer!

As we forgive those done to us,
—The lamb, the linnet, and the hare—

Forgive us all our trespasses,
Little creatures, everywhere!

Splinter _____

Carl Sandburg

The voice of the last cricket
across the first frost
is one kind of good-by.
It is so thin a splinter of singing.

One Day in August

William Stafford

There in the suddenly
  still
    wide street lay
Spot.

No dog so alone
  should
    ever have to mean
That—

    Suddenly forever
    Still.

RESPONDING

1. (a) In the first poem, what "little things" is the poem about? (b) Why do these little things run in fear?

2. Why should we ask the little things to forgive us?

3. (a) In the second poem, to what does the poet compare the voice of the last cricket? (b) Why is this a good comparison?

4. Why is the poem called "Splinter"?

5. In the third poem, what does the dog mean?

WRITING

Part of the joy of creative writing comes from being able to put yourself in someone else's shoes and express this person's thoughts and feelings. Imagine you owned Spot, the dog in "One Day in August." What must you be feeling? What must you be thinking? Write an *elegy*, or poem of mourning, for your dog.

Forget not that the earth delights to feel your bare feet and the winds long to play with your hair.

Kahlil Gibran

Green Places and Other Delights

When you look at a grain of sand, do you see the miracle of creation?

from *Auguries of Innocence* __
William Blake

To see the World in a grain of sand,
And a Heaven in a wild flower,
Hold Infinity in the palm of your hand,
And Eternity in an hour.

RESPONDING

1. (a) What does the poet see in a grain of sand? (b) What does he see in a wildflower?

2. (a) How can infinity be found in the palm of your hand? (b) How can eternity be found in an hour?

WRITING

This poem packs a lot of meaning into four short lines. Think about its theme. Then write another stanza on the same theme continuing the pattern of the poem. Start each line by mentioning something great and end each with something insignificant or tiny.

Does walking in the rain fill you with joy?

Walking in the Rain⎯⎯⎯⎯⎯⎯

Dan Saxon

walking in the rain
the earth has more than
four corners
the earth is a saucer
upside down
i reach for the stars
and pass my arms
through a cloud
i rise off my feet
and hold the moon
against my chest
i caress it and move on
the sun is soon beneath me
and i pick it up and put my
arm through it, and it is a
ring about my muscle
soon i wear it as a wreath
around my neck and smile.

RESPONDING

1. Walking in the rain makes the speaker see the earth in a special way. (a) What metaphor does he use to describe the earth? (b) Do you think this metaphor is a good one? Why or why not?

2. The speaker continues to describe his experience *figuratively;* that is, in language not meant to be taken at face value. (a) What happens when the speaker reaches for the stars? (b) What does he do with the sun?

3. At the end of the poem, why does the speaker smile?

WRITING

Freewrite about an experience you have had of walking in the rain. Then, using figurative language, write a poem expressing your feelings about this experience.

How does daybreak make you feel?

Daybreak in Alabama_____

Langston Hughes

When I get to be a composer
I'm gonna write me some music about
Daybreak in Alabama
And I'm gonna put the purtiest songs in it
Rising out of the ground like a swamp mist
And falling out of heaven like soft dew.
I'm gonna put some tall tall trees in it
And the scent of pine needles
And the smell of red clay after rain
And long red necks
And poppy colored faces
And big brown arms
And the field daisy eyes
Of black and white black white black people
And I'm gonna put white hands
And black hands and brown and yellow hands

RESPONDING

Sensory details appeal to the senses—sight, taste, smell, hearing, and touch. Which details help you experience daybreak in Alabama for yourself?

WRITING

Get up early one morning and experience daybreak for yourself. Jot down your thoughts and feelings. Then, using sensory details, write a poem creating a single impression, or feeling, of daybreak.

How does the coming of spring make you feel?

March

Elizabeth Coatsworth

A blue day,
a blue jay
and a good beginning.

One crow,
melting snow—
spring's winning!

Beyond Winter

Ralph Waldo Emerson

Over the winter glaciers
  I see the summer glow,
And through the wild-piled snowdrift
  The warm rosebuds below.

RESPONDING

1. In the first poem, what impression do the details
   create of March?

2. (a) In the second poem, what does the poet see
   through the snowdrift that shows that winter is
   ending? (b) Do you think that this image is a good
   symbol of winter's ending? Why or why not?

WRITING

Strong images help you say many things in few words.
Using a strong visual image, write a short poem about
winter's ending.

How do you define a perfect day?

Pippa's Passing

Robert Browning

The year's at the spring,
And day's at the morn;
Morning's at seven;
The hill-side's dew-pearl'd;
The lark's on the wing;
The snail's on the thorn;
God's in His Heaven—
All's right with the world!

I Think

James Schuyler

I will write you a letter,
June day. Dear June Fifth,
you're all in green, so
many kinds and all one
green, tree shadows on
grass blades and grass
blade shadows. The air
fills up with motor
mower sound. The cat
walks up the drive
a dead baby rabbit
in her maw. The sun
is hot, the breeze
is cool. And suddenly

in all the green
the lilacs bloom,
massive and exquisite
in color and shape
and scent. The roses
are more full of
buds than ever. No
flowers. But soon.
June day, you have
your own perfection:
so green to say
goodbye to. Green,
stick around
a while.

RESPONDING

1. In the first poem, the speaker begins by telling you the exact time of this poem. What time is it?

2. Even if the speaker had not told you the time, you would have been able to guess it. Which three details indicate this time?

3. Why does the speaker conclude that all is right with the world?

4. In the second poem, what makes the June day perfect?

WRITING

List all the details that make a day seem like heaven to you. Then use these details to write a short poem describing a perfect day.

What makes summer the best season of all?

Knoxville, Tennessee ———

Nikki Giovanni

I always like summer
best
you can eat fresh corn
from daddy's garden
and okra
and greens
and cabbage
and lots of
barbecue
and buttermilk
and homemade ice cream
at the church picnic
and listen to
gospel music

outside
at the church
homecoming
and go to the mountains
with
your grandmother
and go barefooted
and be warm
all the time
not only when you go
to bed
and sleep

RESPONDING

1. (a) Who is the speaker in this poem? (b) Which details tell you this?

2. The speaker provides many reasons for preferring summer. Which reason do you find the most effective? Why?

WRITING

Write a paragraph analyzing the use of imagery in this poem.

What pictures come to mind when you think of winter?

Road
W. S. Merwin

In early snow
going to see a friend
I pass thousands of miles of fences

Sound of Rapids of Laramie River in Late August
W. S. Merwin

White flowers among white stones
under white windy aspens
after night of moonlight and thoughts of snow

RESPONDING

1. (a) In the first poem, does the speaker really pass
   thousands of miles of fences? (b) What makes it seem
   to him as though he does?

2. The second poem describes a scene in late August.
   (a) What is the weather probably like at night near the
   Laramie River? (b) What word does the poet repeat to
   make you think of snow?

WRITING

Both poems create a vivid image in only three lines.
Write a paragraph comparing and contrasting the poems.

Has an unexpected event ever brought about a sudden change in your mood?

Dust of Snow

Robert Frost

The way a crow
Shook down on me
The dust of snow
From a hemlock tree

Has given my heart
A change of mood
And saved some part
Of a day I had rued.

RESPONDING

1. At the beginning of the poem, how does the speaker feel?

2. What changes his mood?

WRITING

Study the pattern of rhythm and rhyme in this poem. Then, following this pattern, write an eight-line poem about an event that brought about a sudden change in your mood.

Do you have your own private special place?

A Green Place _____

William Jay Smith

I know a place all fennel-green and fine
Far from the white icecap, the glacial flaw,
Where shy mud hen and dainty porcupine
Dance in delight by a quivering pawpaw;

Dance by catalpa tree and flowering peach
With speckled guinea fowl and small raccoon,
While the heron, from his perforated beach,
Extends one bony leg beyond the moon.

I know a place so green and fennel-fine
Its boundary is air; and will you come?
A bellflower tinkles by a trumpet vine,
A shrouded cricket taps a midget drum.

There blue flies buzz among the wild sweet peas;
The water speaks: black insects pluck the stream.
May apples cluster there by bearded trees,
Full-skirted dancers risen from a dream.

Birds call; twigs crackle; wild marsh grasses sway;
Will you come soon, before the cold winds blow
To swirl the dust and drive the leaves away,
And thin-ribbed earth pokes out against the snow?

RESPONDING

What does the green place symbolize, or stand for?

WRITING

Alliteration is the repeating of the same initial, or first,
sound in words. Write a paragraph showing how the use
of alliteration gives this poem its musical quality.

121

What gift can wild things give to us?

A Blessing ————————————

James Wright

Just off the highway to Rochester, Minnesota,
Twilight bounds softly forth on the grass.
And the eyes of those two Indian ponies
Darken with kindness.
They have come gladly out of the willows
To welcome my friend and me.
We step over the barbed wire into the pasture
Where they have been grazing all day, alone.
They ripple tensely, they can hardly contain their
    happiness
That we have come.
They bow shyly as wet swans. They love each other.
There is no loneliness like theirs.
At home once more,
They begin munching the young tufts of spring in the
    darkness.
I would like to hold the slenderer one in my arms,
For she has walked over to me
And nuzzled my left hand.
She is black and white,
Her mane falls wild on her forehead,
And the light breeze moves me to caress her long ear
That is delicate as the skin over a girl's wrist.
Suddenly I realize
That if I stepped out of my body I would break
Into blossom.

The Peace of Wild Things _____

Wendell Berry

When despair for the world grows in me
and I wake in the night at the least sound
in fear of what my life and my children's lives may be,
I go and lie down where the wood drake
rests in his beauty on the water, and the great heron
    feeds.
I come into the peace of wild things
who do not tax their lives with forethought
of grief. I come into the presence of still water.
And I feel above me the day-blind stars
waiting with their light. For a time
I rest in the grace of the world, and am free.

RESPONDING

1. A blessing is something sacred, but it is also any gift
   that adds to happiness. (a) What event brings the
   speaker happiness? (b) How is this event sacred?

2. In "The Peace of Wild Things," what lesson does the
   speaker learn from the wild things?

WRITING

We all know the value of gifts such as bicycles,
skateboards, and computers. Some gifts, though, are more
intangible, or unable to be seen or clearly identified.
Freewrite about one of these intangible gifts. Then, using
free verse, turn your freewriting into a poem.

Do some people go through life asleep to their senses?

The Waking _____

Theodore Roethke

I strolled across
An open field;
The sun was out;
Heat was happy.

This way! This way!
The wren's throat
  shimmered,
Either to other,
The blossoms sang.

The stones sang,
The little ones did,
And flowers jumped
Like small goats.

A ragged fringe
Of daisies waved;

I wasn't alone
In a grove of apples.
Far in the wood
A nestling sighed;
The dew loosened
Its morning smells.

I came where the river
Ran over stones:
My ears knew
An early joy.

And all the waters
Of all the streams
Sang in my veins
That summer day.

RESPONDING

1. In this poem, the speaker awakes to his senses. Which sensory details did you find most effective? Why?

2. How do all these details make the speaker feel?

WRITING

Write a paragraph examining the use of sensory details in this poem.

What image does fog create in your mind?

Fog —— Fog ——
Carl Sandburg
William Jay Smith

The fog comes
on little cat feet.

It sits looking
over harbor and city
on silent haunches
and then moves on.

FOG COMES ON HUGE ELEPHANT FEET
RISING UP FROM THE RIVER SWING-
ING DOWN EACH BLACK ABANDONED
STREET CRASHING THROUGH TREES
CRUMPLING STEEL GATES AND TELE-
PHONE POLES UPROOTING RAILROAD
TIES AND BILLBOARDS WRAPPING ITS
TRUNK AROUND THE DOOMED CITY

RESPONDING

1. A *metaphor* is a comparison between two basically
   unlike things. (a) In the first poem, to what does the
   poet compare the fog? (b) What impression does this
   comparison create? In other words, how does it make
   you feel about the fog?

2. (a) In the second poem, to what does the poet compare
   the fog? (b) What impression does this comparison
   create?

3. Why do you think William Jay Smith used all capital
   letters in his poem?

WRITING

Choose one of the following subjects: rain, thunder,
dawn, nightfall, sunshine, lightning. Write a short poem
comparing this subject to an animal.

Has fog ever filled you with delight?

The quiet fog

Marge Piercy

The pitch pines fade
into a whiteness
that has blotted the marsh.

Beyond
starts ten feet
outside the magic circle
of lit house.

The hill has dissolved.
The road ends

under a soft wall
that creeps.

Why am I happy?
I cradle my elbows
corners of a mirror
tall as childhood
reflecting
nothing.

RESPONDING

1. How does the fog make the lit house appear?

2. What effect does it have on the hill?

3. What is the "soft wall that creeps"?

4. Why is the speaker happy?

WRITING

Some of us enjoy snuggling up with a good book on a
rainy afternoon. Others like to look at a snowstorm from
behind a frost-covered window. What special weather
condition gives you particular pleasure? For example, it
might be a hurricane, a thunderstorm, or a blizzard.
Write a short poem describing this condition and the
feelings it stirs up in you.

Do you take pleasure from living in the city?

The City ───────────────────
David Ignatow

If flowers want to grow
right out of the concrete sidewalk cracks
I'm going to bend down and smell them.

City ─────────────────────────
Langston Hughes

In the morning the city
Spreads its wings
Making a song
In stone that sings.

In the evening the city
Goes to bed
Hanging lights
About its head.

RESPONDING

1. In the first poem, the flowers seem to have a will of their own. They decide where they will grow. Why will the speaker bend down and smell the flowers?

2. In the second poem, the poet first pictures the city as a bird. In what way is it like a bird?

3. The poet then pictures the city as a person. In what way is it like a person?

WRITING

Who does the city seem most like to you: a boxer, a ballerina, a truck driver, a jogger? Choose one of these people or come up with your own person. Then write a poem presenting the city as this person.

*E*nter these enchanted woods,
You who dare.

George Meredith

That Enchanted Kingdom

Do you find magic in everyday life?

Otherwise

Aileen Fisher

There must be magic:
Otherwise,
How could day turn to night?
And how could sailboats,
Otherwise,
Go sailing out of sight?
And how could peanuts,
Otherwise,
Be covered up so tight?

Witchcraft was hung, in History

Emily Dickinson

Witchcraft was hung, in History,
But History and I
Find all the Witchcraft that we need
Around us, every Day—

The White Horse _____

D. H. Lawrence

The youth walks up to the white horse, to put its halter
 on
and the horse looks at him in silence.
They are so silent they are in another world.

RESPONDING

1. In "Otherwise," what three examples does the poet give
   of magic in everyday life?

2. Usually we think of magic in terms of the
   supernatural. In what way does Fisher's definition
   seem to be different from the usual definition?

3. (a) What does Dickinson mean when she says,
   "Witchcraft was hung, in History"? (b) Where does she
   find witchcraft?

4. In what way is "The White Horse" also about magic in
   everyday life?

WRITING

Brainstorm with your classmates. Form a list of examples
of magic in everyday life. Select the examples you think
the best. Then write a short poem about magic.

Did you ever dream of a magical kingdom?

from **Kubla Khan**

Samuel Taylor Coleridge

A damsel with a dulcimer
In a vision once I saw:
It was an Abyssian maid,
And on her dulcimer she played,
Singing of Mount Abora.
Could I revive within me
Her symphony and song,
To such a deep delight 'twould win me,
That with music loud and long,
I would build that dome on air,
That sunny dome! those caves of ice!
And all who heard should see them there,
And all should cry, Beware! Beware!
His flashing eyes, his floating hair!
Weave a circle round him thrice,
And close your eyes with holy dread.
For he on honey-dew hath fed,
And drunk the milk of Paradise.

RESPONDING

1. Why would the people who see the poet shout "Beware"?

2. In what way would the poet have seen Paradise?

WRITING

Imagine you are the damsel playing her dulcimer, a type of stringed instrument. Write the song you sang.

Can beauty itself be enchanted?

Sleeping Beauty

Walter De La Mare

The scent of bramble fills the air,
Amid her folded sheets she lies,
The gold of evening in her hair,
The blue of morn shut in her eyes.

How many a changing moon hath lit
The unchanging roses of her face!
Her mirror ever broods on it
In silver stillness of the days.

Oft flits the moth on filmy wings
Into his solitary lair;
Shrill evensong the cricket sings
From some still shadow in her hair.

In heat, in snow, in wind, in flood,
She sleeps in lovely loneliness,
Half-folded like an April bud
On winter-haunted trees.

RESPONDING

Read again the last four lines. What is the meaning of
the simile?

WRITING

Many fairy tales deal with enchanted beings, or beings
who are under magical spells. List as many of these
enchanted beings from fairy tales as you can. Then select
one and write a short poem telling this person's story.

Can an enchantment bring pain and sorrow?

La Belle Dame sans Merci___

John Keats

O what can ail thee, knight-at-arms,
  Alone and palely loitering?
The sedge has withered from the lake,
  And no birds sing.

O what can ail thee, knight-at-arms,
  So haggard and so woe-begone?
The squirrel's granary is full,
  And the harvest's done.

I see a lily on thy brow
  With anguish moist and fever dew,
And on thy cheek a fading rose
  Fast withereth too.

I met a lady in the meads,
  Full beautiful—a faery's child;
Her hair was long, her foot was light,
  And her eyes were wild.

I made a garland for her head,
  And bracelets too, and fragrant zone;
She looked at me as she did love,
  And made sweet moan.

I set her on my pacing steed,
  And nothing else saw all day long,
For sidelong would she bend, and sing
  A faery's song.

She found me roots of relish sweet,
  And honey wild, and manna dew,
And sure in language strange she said—
  "I love thee true!"

She took me to her elfin grot,
  And there she wept and sighed full sore,
And there I shut her wild wild eyes
  With kisses four.

And there she lulléd me asleep,
  And there I dreamed—and woe betide!
The latest dream I ever dreamed
  On the cold hill side.

I saw pale kings and princes too,
  Pale warriors, death-pale were they all;
They cried—"La Belle Dame sans Merci
  Hath thee in thrall!"

I saw their starvéd lips in the gloam,
  With horrid warning gaped wide,
And I awoke and found me here,
  On the cold hill's side.

And this is why I sojourn here,
  Alone and palely loitering,
Though the sedge has withered from the lake
  And no birds sing.

RESPONDING

1. La Bell Dame sans Merci is the beautiful lady without mercy. Where does the knight first meet this lady?

2. (a) Why is the knight now filled with woe? (b) Why do no birds sing?

WRITING

A *narrative poem* tells a story. Write a paragraph paraphrasing, or telling in different words, the story told by this poem.

Have you ever felt that you were living in two worlds at once?

Independent Testimony _____

Charles Simic

How strange to overhear oneself
Say *I*
At four in the morning
Alive alive
A needle in the great haystack
Here and not here
By the wide open window
Under some dim constellation
A feeling granted everyone
Of living in two worlds
One of which is unsayable

RESPONDING

1. How does the speaker feel at four o'clock in the morning?

2. What are the two worlds he feels he is living in?

3. Which of these two worlds is unsayable? Why?

WRITING

Have you ever awakened suddenly at an unusual hour and been unable to go back to sleep? Freewrite about the feelings you have had at this hour. Then write a short poem about this experience.

Does every story have two sides?

Interview

Sara Henderson Hay

Yes, this is where she lived before she won
The title Miss Glass Slipper of the Year,
And went to the ball and married the king's son.
You're from the local press, and want to hear
About her early life? Young man, sit down.
These are my *own* two daughters; you'll not find
Nicer, more biddable girls in all the town,
And lucky, I tell them, not to be the kind

That Cinderella was, spreading those lies,
Telling those shameless tales about the way
We treated her. Oh, nobody denies
That she was pretty, if you like those curls.
But looks aren't everything, I always say.
Be sweet and natural, I tell my girls,
And Mr. Right will come along, some day.

RESPONDING

1. Who is the speaker in this poem?

2. In what way does the speaker present a different side
   of the Cinderella story?

WRITING

Point of view is the angle from which a story is told.
Write a poem telling a familiar story from an unusual
point of view. For example, you might decide to tell the
tale of the three little pigs from the wolf's point of view.

Have you ever been overcome by a sense of strangeness?

Haiku

Translated from the Japanese by Harry Behn

Once upon a time
there was, and is, an old witch . . .
a dry tuft of grass.

Issa

That duck, bobbing up
from the green deeps of a pond,
has seen something strange . . .

Joso

RESPONDING

1. Why does the duck bob up?

WRITING

Haiku is a form of Japanese lyric poetry. It creates a vivid image of something that has moved the poet. Haiku is written in seventeen syllables. The first line contains five syllables; the second, seven; and the last, five.

Think about sights that have moved you. Then write your own haiku.

Can we reach each other over long distances?

Long Distance _____

William Stafford

Sometimes when you watch the fire
ashes glow and gray
the way the sun turned cold on spires
in winter in the town back home
so far away.

Sometimes on the telephone
the one you hear goes far
and ghostly voices whisper in.
You think they are from other wires.
You think they are.

RESPONDING

1. What happens sometimes when you watch the fire?

2. What happens sometimes when you speak on the telephone?

3. *Telepathy* is the ability to communicate over long distances through means that are not known to science. In what way is this poem about telepathy?

WRITING

Write a paragraph analyzing the mood of this poem.

Can the wind uncover a secret?

The Secret _____

James Stephens

I was frightened, for a wind
Crept along the grass, to say
Something that was in my mind
Yesterday—

Something that I did not know
Could be found out by the wind;
I had buried it so low
In my mind!

RESPONDING

1. Why is the speaker frightened?

2. A secret is something private or kept hidden. From whom has the speaker kept his secret?

3. A secret is also a mystery, or something beyond understanding. How is this poem itself a secret?

WRITING

Write a paragraph analyzing the theme of this poem.

Have you ever felt a place was haunted?

Southern Mansion

Arna Bontemps

Poplars are standing there still as death
and ghosts of dead men
meet their ladies walking
two by two beneath the shade
and standing on the marble steps.

There is a sound of music echoing
through the open door
and in the field there is
another sound tinkling in the cotton:
chains of bondmen dragging on the ground.

The years go back with an iron clank,
a hand is on the gate,
a dry leaf trembles on the wall.
Ghosts are walking.
They have broken roses down
and poplars stand there still as death.

RESPONDING

According to folk legend, places are haunted because the
dead who once lived there cannot rest. Why is this
southern mansion haunted?

WRITING

List the details in this poem that help create a vivid
picture of a haunted place. Then write your own poem
describing a haunting.

*Have you ever walked among ruins and felt the ghosts
of the people who once lived there?*

The Island of Yorrick _____

N. M. Bodecker

The island of Yorrick
is intensely historic,
and covered with ruins
Ionic and Doric.
The people who live there
are phantasmagoric,
which means: There are ghosts
on the island of Yorrick.

RESPONDING

1. Why does the island of Yorrick seem haunted?

2. What is the tone of this poem?

WRITING

In this poem, the poet has fun playing with rhymes.
Write a paragraph explaining how the use of rhyme helps
convey the tone.

Does your pulse quicken as the end of October approaches?

All Hallows

Louise Glück

Even now this landscape is assembling.
The hills darken. The oxen
sleep in their blue yoke,
the fields having been
picked clean, the sheaves
bound evenly and piled at the roadside
among cinquefoil, as the toothed moon rises:

This is the barrenness
of harvest or pestilence.
And the wife leaning out the window
with her hand extended, as in payment,
and the seeds
distinct, gold, calling
Come here
Come here, little one

And the soul creeps out of the tree.

RESPONDING

All Hallows is a holiday celebrating the dead. Halloween
stems from this holiday. Which details in this poem fill
you with a sense of foreboding, or evil about to happen?

WRITING

This poem leaves you with a very unsettled feeling.
Normal, everyday things seem to be cast in an evil light.
Write a paragraph telling the effect this poem has on you.

Have you ever heard footsteps on the stairs in the middle of the night?

Night-Piece

Raymond R. Patterson

I do not sleep at night.
Rain does not lull me, and the withered wind
Is always out of tune, when there is wind
Or moon enough for light.

The sounds, up from the street,
Fall back again, unclaimed: The dispossessed
Call out with longing to the dispossessed.
The sounds repeat, repeat . . .

But never call my name;
Though I have heard the footsteps mount the stair,
The steady tread that echoes down the stair—
And trembled just the same . . .

As if someone had come
But could not find me, passing by my room,
And did not know I waited in my room,
Lonely, sleepless and dumb.

RESPONDING

Why does the speaker not sleep at night?

WRITING

Sleepless nights are often filled with their own special mixture of loneliness and fear. Write a poem expressing your feelings during a sleepless time.

How can a common, everyday bird strike terror in the heart?

from **The Raven**

Edgar Allan Poe

And the Raven, never flitting, still is sitting, *still* is
    sitting
On the pallid bust of Pallas just above my chamber door;
And his eyes have all the seeming of a demon's that is
    dreaming,
And the lamp-light o'er him streaming throws his shadow
    on the floor;
And my soul from out that shadow that lies floating on
    the floor

Shall be lifted—nevermore!

Poem

Southwest Tribes

There came a gray owl at sunset,
there came a gray owl at sunset,
hooting softly around me.
He brought terror to my heart.

RESPONDING

How are the raven and the owl alike?

WRITING

Rhyme can occur at the ends of lines, but it also can occur within lines. Look again at the first poem. Write a paragraph explaining the rhyme scheme in these lines.

Does the unknown and unknowable fill you with fear?

Something Is There _____

Lilian Moore

Something is there
   there on the stair
     coming down
       coming down
         stepping with care.
      Coming down
        coming down
          slinkety-sly.

Something is coming and wants to get by.

Fear _____

Charles Simic

Fear passes from man to man
Unknowing,
As one leaf passes its shudder
To another.

All at once the whole tree is trembling
And there is no sign of the wind.

146

Moon Tiger

Denise Levertov

The moon tiger.
In the room, here.
It came in, it is
prowling sleekly
under and over
the twin beds.
See its small head,
silver smooth,
hear the pad of its
large feet. Look,
its white stripes
in the light that slid
through the jalousies.
It is sniffing our
clothes, its cold nose
nudges our bodies.
The beds are narrow,
but I'm coming in with you.

RESPONDING

1. The lines in a poem can be arranged to create a picture. How do the lines in the first poem look like what the poem is about?

2. (a) In the second poem, what simile does the poet use to describe the way fear passes from person to person? (b) Do you think this simile is a good one? Why or why not?

3. In the third poem, the poet uses a metaphor to describe the way the moon comes into the room. (a) To what does she compare the moon? (b) Do you think this metaphor is a good one? Why or why not?

WRITING

Both "Something Is There" and "Moon Tiger" contain several words beginning with the letter *s*. Read each poem aloud. Write a paragraph explaining how the repetition of the letter *s* helps create the mood of each poem.

Do you know a magical place?

Where the Sidewalk Ends ____

Shel Silverstein

There is a place where the sidewalk ends
And before the street begins,
And there the grass grows soft and white,
And there the sun burns crimson bright,
And there the moon-bird rests from his flight
To cool in the peppermint wind.

Let us leave this place where the smoke blows black
And the dark street winds and bends.
Past the pits where the asphalt flowers grow
We shall walk with a walk that is measured and slow,
And watch where the chalk-white arrows go
To the place where the sidewalk ends.

Yes we'll walk with a walk that is measured and slow,
And we'll go where the chalk-white arrows go,
For the children, they mark, and the children, they know
The place where the sidewalk ends.

RESPONDING

1. How is the place where the poet is, different from the place where the sidewalk ends?

2. Why do children know where the sidewalk ends?

WRITING

Imagine you found the place where the sidewalk ends. Write a short poem telling about what you see there.

150